OPEN COCKPITS & STRAW BALES

OPEN COCKPITS & STRAW BALES

Motor Racing in the 1950s

BRYAN APPS

HALSGROVE

First published in Great Britain in 2011

British Library Cataloguing-in-Publication Data
A CIP record for this title is available from the British Library

ISBN 978 0 85704 112 8

HALSGROVE
Halsgrove House,
Ryelands Business Park,
Bagley Road, Wellington, Somerset TA21 9PZ
Tel: 01823 653777   Fax: 01823 216796
email: sales@halsgrove.com

Part of the Halsgrove group of companies.
Information on all Halsgrove titles is available at: www.halsgrove.com

Printed in China by Everbest Printing Co Ltd

CONTENTS

Introduction 9

Motor racing after the war 14

1950   The dominance of the 158 Alfa Romeo 17

1951   Juan Fangio establishes his mastery 33

1952   The unrivalled Ferrari 500 47

1953   The A6SSG Maserati joins the party 65

1954   A display of Teutonic thoroughness 78

1955   The triumph and tragedy of the Silver Arrows 94

1956   The emergence of the Lancia-Ferrari 109

1957   A very British Grand Prix 122

1958   A British World Champion at last 134

1959   The shape of things to come 147

The end of the decade 159

BIBLIOGRAPHY

Motor Sport; Autosport; Motoring News; Grand Prix by Trevor R Griffiths; *Grand Prix!* by Mike Lang; *Stirling Moss* by Stirling Moss with Doug Nye; *Stirling Moss – the Champion Without a Crown* by Pierre Menard and Jacques Vassal; *All My Races* by Stirling Moss and Alan Henry; *Famous Racing Cars* by Doug Nye; *The Concise Encyclopaedia of Formula One* by David Tremayne and Mark Hughes; *With Flying Colours* by LJK Setright, Derek Forsyth and Robert Newman; *Formula One Unseen Archives* by Tim Hill; *Ferrari* by Hans Tanner with Doug Nye; *Ferrari – the Grand Prix Cars* by Alan Henry; *British Grand Prix* by Maurice Hamilton; *BRM* by Raymond Mays with Peter Roberts; *The Shelsley Walsh Story* by Simon Taylor; *A History of the World's Racing Cars* by Richard Hough and Michael Frostick; *Classic Racing Cars* by Nye and Goddard; *Track Pass* by Geoff Goddard with Doug Nye; *Mom Ami Mate* by Chris Nixon; *Stirling Moss* by Robert Edwards; *The Golden Age of Motor Racing* by Tim Hill; *Formula 1* by Rainer W Schlegelmilch and Hartmut Lehbrink; *British Cars at Le Mans* by Dominique Pascal; *101 Brockbank Cartoons* with forward by Quentin Blake .

Thanks are due to Colin Simmons and Grant Wells for their help in the compilation of this book.

INTRODUCTION

IT WAS A great time to be British. We had just won the war, with a little help from our friends, and we were to celebrate both the Festival of Britain and the Coronation, conquer Everest, run the first four minute mile, and produce the world's first jet airliner. The 1950s was also a great time to be a motor racing enthusiast. It would have been good to have watched my dear friend Manfred von Brauchitsch taking on Bernd Rosemayer and Tazio Nuvolari in the 1930s, but I became a teenager in 1950 and there was plenty to fuel my enthusiasm then too. To begin with there were the Alfa Romeos and E.R.A.s, dusted off after six years of enforced rest, and in 1952 the brief appearance of Hermann Lang in a 1939 Grand Prix Mercedes in Argentina. Entirely new racing cars were being crafted in England, Italy and France in what was little more than a cottage industry and, also in the 1950s, Jaguar and Aston Martin echoed the epic victories of the 'Bentley Boys' at Le Mans.

Hermann Lang's 1939 W154/163 3 litre Grand Prix Mercedes Benz finishing second to Froilan Gonzales' Ferrari in the 1951 Presidente Peron Grand Prix in Buenos Aires.

Dennis Poore setting the
Fastest Time of the Day at
Shelsley Walsh in his 1936 V12
3.8 litre supercharged Alfa
Romeo in 1950.

In the years immediately after the war racing cars were still operated by controls which any motorist would easily recognise today. Racing drivers were clearly visible in their open cockpits, often with only thin leather helmets to protect their heads. National colours and large racing numbers made the cars and their drivers easy to identify as they sped past only yards away from where one stood.

The 4CLT Maserati looked exactly how a racing car ought to look and the big 4.5 litre Ferraris and Lago Talbots were mightily spectacular. H.W.M.s led the way from Britain to

Stirling Moss driving the two
seater H.W.M. Alta at Garda
on 15 October 1950.

the Continental circuits, and in 1950 Raymond Mays struck a chord with the whole nation with the B.R.M. He intended it to be a world beater and it certainly sounded like a winner whenever it could be persuaded to fire on all 16 cylinders. The B.R.M. drew vast swathes of the British public to motor racing for the first time, and my correspondence with Raymond Mays and Alfred Owen enabled me to feel uniquely in touch with the sport. John Cooper's little 500cc racers brought added interest and excitement to any race meeting and within ten years he produced the World Championship winning 2.5 litre Cooper-Climax. Such was the speed of change in Formula 1 in the course of the 1950s. H.W.M.s were joined in Formula 2 by Connaughts, Cooper-Bristols and Gordinis, and chance catapulted John Heath, Rodney Clark, John Cooper and Amede Gordini into the World Championship series in 1952. The 1950s also produced flights of fancy like the 'Toothpaste Tube' Connaught, and adventurous projects such as the transverse engined Bugatti. Space frames gave birth to the iconic 250F Maserati, the exciting D50 Lancia, the W196 Mercedes Benz, and the Vanwalls. The 2.5 litre B.R.M., equipped with a space frame but almost a monocoque, eventually became a Grand Prix winner at Zandvoort in 1959. There was also the front-engined Lotus and the beautifully constructed Aston Martin DBR4 which, like the original B.R.M., arrived too late to make an impact.

In the 1950s a works Aston Martin was actually driven along the public roads of England and France to compete at Le Mans. The astonishingly graceful XK120 Jaguar of William Lyons gained instant success on the track and was followed in quick succession by the C Type and the D Type Jaguars. Each year new models appeared so that, for example, the David Brown Aston Martins progressed in rapid stages from the sports saloon DB1, via the DB3 and the curvaceous DB3S to the Le Mans winning DBR1. Ferrari and Maserati produced new cars annually, and the gull winged 300SL Mercedes caused the motor racing

Stirling Moss winning Heat 2 of the Brands Hatch Open Challenge Race in his Cooper-Norton in 1950.

Sidney Allard setting a new
record in his J2 Allard during
the Brighton Speed Trials in
1950.

world to draw its breath at Le Mans in 1952. Also not to be forgotten were the Chrysler
engined Allards and the succession of sports racing cars which Briggs Cunningham brought
to Le Mans each year from the United States.

Then there were the drivers. Young British drivers such as Stirling Moss, Tony Brooks,
Mike Hawthorn and Peter Collins who, had they been born a few years earlier, might have
flown Spitfires and Hurricanes in the Battle of Britain, but who instead faced perils which
were real enough in their magnificent machines with which they all but flew around the
most demanding of circuits. They were incredibly brave, fully knowing that the smallest
error or mechanical defect could cost them their lives. Sadly, Peter Collins was killed when
his Dino Ferrari shot off the road at speed during the 1958 German Grand Prix at the
Nurburgring, while Mike Hawthorn who, having retired from racing was still addicted to
speed, died in the mangled wreckage of his 3.4 litre Jaguar on the Guildford bypass after
showing Rob Walker's 300SL Mercedes a clean pair of heels.

Then there were the great Italian drivers like Alberto Ascari, Giuseppe Farina, Eugenio
Castellotti and Luigi Musso, and the universally acknowledged Argentinian maestro Juan
Fangio. They drove their fabulous cars on circuits that were lined by stout trees, unforgiving
walls, and spectators who occasionally even ventured on to the course itself. Each race could
easily have proved to be their last, and too frequently was but, as I have often been assured
by the drivers themselves, danger was part of the thrill for them and the spectators alike.

In the 1950s the Monte Carlo Rally was an important annual event which really counted.
It was often a battle against the elements with snow, ice and fog preventing many of the
entrants from making it across the Alps to Monaco. The Mille Miglia was the last of the
great inter city road races and it was justly considered to be the ultimate test of men and
machines.

There were many high points, such as the race-long dual between Juan Fangio's Maserati
and Mike Hawthorn's Ferrari in the 1953 French Grand Prix; the epic victory of Tony
Brooks in his Connaught at Syracuse in 1955; and that of Stirling Moss and Denis Jenkinson

in the 1955 Mille Miglia. The lowest point was the tragic accident at Le Mans in 1955 when Pierre Levegh's 300SLR Mercedes, in avoiding Hawthorn's D Type Jaguar, hit Lance Macklin's Austin Healey and destroyed itself at the cost of eighty-two lives.

So many great racing drivers lost their lives in the course of those ten years and all of them are remembered here. This book inevitably majors on the Formula 1 World Championship series which began at Silverstone in 1950, but some notable non championship events are also included and, in addition, the Monte Carlo Rally, the Mille Miglia and Le Mans. The accounts of all these events are inevitably brief, but also, hopefully, informative, and I have enjoyed bringing colour to the images of the 1950s, many of which have only previously been recorded in black and white.

MOTOR RACING
AFTER THE WAR

THE LAST MOTOR race to take place before the Second World War was held on 3 September 1939, the very day on which Britain and France declared war on Germany. It was the Yugoslav Grand Prix in Belgrade and it was won by Tarzio Nuvolari in a 3 litre supercharged D Type Auto Union. Manfred von Brauchitsch came second in a W154/163 Mercedes Benz and Hermann Muller third in another Auto Union. After this all the racing cars fell silent for the duration of the war but it was not long after the hostilities ended that motor racing resumed again. The first race took place in Paris on 9 September 1945 and it was won by Jean-Pierre Wimille who roared down the Bois de Boulogne in a 1939 4.7 litre supercharged Bugatti. However the cars which dominated motor racing in the years immediately after the war were the 1.5 litre supercharged 158 Alfa Romeos which had been designed by Gioacchino Colombo. In 1938 they had been intended for Voiturette races but, after being hidden in a cheese factory for the duration, they emerged to take on the 4CL Maseratis, Talbots, Delahayes and British E.R.A.s on more than equal terms.

In 1946 the International Association of Recognised Automobile Clubs became the Federation International de l'Automobile or FIA, and decided to adopt Formula Libre for Grands Prix to enable pre war racing cars of every description to race against each other. It meant, for example, that Raymond Sommer was able to pit his 3 litre supercharged 1938 Alfa Romeo against cars with only half its engine capacity. Racing resumed in England on a more modest scale that year with Raymond Mays putting up the fastest time of the day in his E.R.A. both at Shelsley Walsh in June and in the Brighton and Hove Motor Club Speed Trial along the seafront in September.

In 1947 the FIA decreed that only cars of up to 1.5 litres supercharged and 4.5 litres unsupercharged would be eligible for Grand Prix events and so prepared the way for the first World Championship three years later. The British Racing Drivers' Club organised the British Empire Trophy Race in St Helier Jersey on 8 May and it was won by Reg Parnell in a 4CL Maserati, watched by people who leaned over their garden gates as he sped down their roads.

The first post war race to justify being called a Grand Prix was the Swiss Grand Prix which was held on 8 June 1947 at Berne. Spectators crowded along the grass verge at the side of the circuit, their toes often on the road itself, to watch the 158 Alfa Romeos of Jean-Pierre Wimille, Archille Varzi and Count Carlo Trossi claim the first three places in the Final. The Alfas occupied the first four places in the European Grand Prix at Spa but, in their absence,

Louis Chiron was able to win the Lyons Grand Prix in his 4.5 litre unsupercharged Lago Talbot. The Maseratis of Luigi Villoresi, Alberto Ascari and Baron Emmanuel de Graffenried all lost time during the race at Lyons through having to stop for fuel.

In 1948 Adolfo Orsi produced the 4CLT Maserati, which was in effect a 4CL with a tubular chassis, and it became known as the San Remo after winning the San Remo Grand Prix in the hands of Alberto Ascari on June 27. Alfa Romeo stayed away from the revived Monaco Grand Prix that year and the race was won by Giuseppe Farina in a Maserati from Louis Chiron's Lago Talbot, a post war French Simca Gordini finishing in fourth place. The Alfa Romeos of Trossi and Wimille won the European Grand Prix, Varzi having been killed in practice before the race, and the Alfas took the first three places at Rheims. Three entirely new 1.5 litre supercharged 12 cylinder Tipo 125 Ferraris made their debut in 1948 but, disappointingly, proved no match for the Alfa Romeos which, at the re opened Monza circuit, took the first four places in the hands of Wimille, Trossi, Consalvo Sanesi, and Piero Taruffi. The Alfas missed the Penya Rhin race in Spain and this allowed the honours to go to the 4CLT Maseratis of Luigi Villoresi and Reg Parnell.

Both Brooklands and Donington Park had suffered as a result of being requisitioned for military purposes during the war and so the aerodrome circuit of Silverstone was chosen as the venue for the first British Grand Prix on October 2 1948. Alfa Romeo stayed away, having no more to prove, and Bob Gerard came third in his beautifully prepared E.R.A. to the 4CLT Maseratis of Luigi Villoresi and Alberto Ascari.

Content to sit on its laurels, Alfa Romeo withdrew from motor racing altogether in 1949 and Juan Fangio won the San Remo Grand Prix in a 4CLT Maserati painted in the Argentinian colours of blue and yellow. The Belgian Grand Prix at Spa proved to be Louis Rosier's greatest win, driving his Lago Talbot, but it was Ferrari's turn to receive the laurels

Louis Chiron winning the 1949 French Grand Prix at Rheims in his Lago Talbot.

next in Berne with Prince Bira and Villoresi leading Sommer's Lago Talbot across the line. The V12 1.5 litre supercharged Ferrari Tipo 125 had found reliability through the use of Vandervell Thinwall bearings, and this was to enable Tony Vandervell to buy green Ferraris with which to go motor racing. Louis Chiron was the popular winner at Rheims in his Lago Talbot but Villoresi won the Dutch Grand Prix in an improved Ferrari with a two stage supercharged engine and a longer wheelbase which improved its handling. Then Ascari gave Enzo Ferrari the win that most mattered to him at Monza in the European Grand Prix. The second British Grand Prix, held again at Silverstone, went to Baron de Graffenried's 4CLT Maserati with Bob Gerard's E.R.A. second and Louis Rosier's Lago Talbot third.

By the end of the 1940s motor racing had become firmly re-established in Europe, in spite of the absence of the great German teams and with no racing cars from England capable of competing on equal terms with the Italians. Yet there was plenty of interest for the enthusiast and the first meeting on the Battle of Britain aerodrome circuit of Westhampnett took place on 18 September 1948. Looking back now, my first Goodwood race meeting on 18 April 1949 was a very British affair and even the 4CLT Maseratis entered by the Scuderia Ambrosiana were driven by the Englishmen, Reg Parnell and Fred Ashmore. The facilities were rudimentary but the crowd was generally good natured and well informed. There was a varied assortment of cars competing in a series of short races and, in spite of the rain, it was a good day out for all. Apart from the ten-lap Richmond Trophy Race all the events were run over just five laps to ensure that some cars at any rate would still be running at the end. A five lap race was held mainly for 500cc Cooper Nortons and Cooper J.A.P.s driven by Stirling Moss, Peter Collins, Spike Rhiando and others, but the legendary Don Parker, minus underwear to lighten his load, came home third in his one-off Parker C.F.S. There was a race for unsupercharged cars up to 2 litres which featured M.G.s, Rileys, an H.R.G. and an HW Alta; three handicap races designed to make it theoretically possible for all the widely disparate cars to cross the line together, and the Chichester Cup and Richmond Trophy races for Grand Prix cars. The flame red 4CLT Maserati of Reg Parnell excelled, as it had the previous September, but there were other Maseratis, an Alfa Romeo, a Delage, and numerous E.R.A.s from the 1930s to add to the spectacle.

With Alfa Romeo dominating motor races throughout Europe and Enzo Ferrari preparing to make a strong challenge, three ambitious projects were launched elsewhere in an effort to wrest from Italy its apparent stranglehold on motor racing.

The clinically named Type 360 was designed by Professor von Eberhorst and Dr Ferry Porsche, both of whom had been largely responsible for the D Type Auto Union. It was built by Cisitalia in Turin and its flat 12 1.5 litre supercharged engine was situated behind the driver. The car had a multi-tubular space frame and was years ahead of its time, but the project ran out of funds and it never actually raced.

The C.T.A. Arsenal had the backing of the French Government and the car, which was designed by Lory who had been responsible for the 1930 Delage, had a 1.5 litre V8 engine with two stage superchargers. Sadly this project also failed to progress beyond its development stage.

In Britain Raymond Mays and Peter Berthon who, with Humphrey Cook had produced the E.R.A. before the war, set out to create a world beating Grand Prix contender with their 1.5 litre supercharged 16 cylinder B.R.M. If enthusiasm had been all that was required to achieve success the car would have been a winner and Mays persuaded 200 British firms to contribute to his project. The design was too ambitious and complex and when it had been developed to the point at which, in terms of sheer power and reliability, it might have achieved what its designer had intended, it was too late because the Grand Prix circus had moved on. Yet, at the beginning of 1950, where the account in this book really begins, great things were expected of the B.R.M. which was set to make its debut in that year.

1950
The dominance of the 158 Alfa Romeo

1950 marked a milestone in the history of motor racing as it was the year in which the World Championship for drivers was established. It had been decided that the first five finishers in each race would be awarded 8, 6, 4, 3, 2 points respectively, and that a further point would be allotted to the driver establishing the fastest lap of the race. If a driver handed his car over to a team mate in the course of the race the points would be divided between the two of them. In 1950 the races which counted towards the Championship were held at Silverstone, Monaco, Berne, Spa, Rheims and Monza, with the addition of the Indianapolis 500 Race in America to help justify its claim to world status. The cars competing in the European events had to conform to the 1.5 litre supercharged/ 4.5litre unsupercharged formula, and it was essential that the 158 Alfa Romeos should be persuaded to return so that the Series could truthfully be said to represent the very best. The Alfa Romeo team won all six of the European races, and an improved 159 model appeared late in the year at Monza with more power and a De Dion rear axle. In fact, Alfa drivers were to take the first three places in the new World Championship. Ferrari introduced the Tipo 375 at Spa with a 3.322cc unsupercharged V12 engine designed by Aurelio Lampredi and, as the season progressed, the Ferrari's engine size was increased, first to 4080cc and then to the maximum 4.5 litres. Privately entered 4CLT Maseratis found themselves to be outclassed in this company but were nevertheless a joy to watch, as were the Lago Talbots. Anthony Lago had managed to increase the power from his 6 cylinder engines which had the advantage of being much less thirsty than the blown Alfas. The perpendicular E.R.A.s made occasional appearances as did the new Simca Gordinis and Altas. The absent guest in 1950, as far as the World Championship series was concerned, was the much vaunted B.R.M., although the car was demonstrated by Raymond Mays at Silverstone on May 13 prior to the British Grand Prix and inspected by King George VI, Queen Elizabeth, Princess Margaret and the Earl and Countess Mountbatten. In the non Championship Daily Express Trophy Race at Silverstone on August 26 the B.R.M. ignominiously sheered a half shaft on the starting line but in some measure redeemed itself at Goodwood on 27 September winning the short Woodcote Cup and Goodwood Trophy races in the hands of Reg Parnell.

Dr Giuseppe Farina

THE WORLD CHAMPIONSHIP SEASON
The British Grand Prix. Silverstone: May 13

Silverstone was given the honour of staging the first Grand Prix in the World Championship series and it also had the distinction of being called the Grand Prix d'Europe. In the absence of the Ferrari team, the 158 Alfa Romeos were clearly in a class of their own. The drivers could be identified by the coloured cowls of their cars, blue for Dr Guiseppe Farina, white for Luigi Fagioli, yellow and blue for Juan Fangio, green for Reg Parnell, and they occupied the entire front row of the starting grid.

The Starting Grid

R. Parnell	J.M. Fangio	L. Fagioli	G. Farina
Alfa Romeo	Alfa Romeo	Alfa Romeo	Alfa Romeo
1 min 52.2 secs	1 min 51.0 secs	1 min 51.0 secs	1 min 50.8 secs

E. Martin	Y.G-Cabantous	B. Bira
Lago Talbot	Lago Talbot	Maserati
1 min 55.4 secs	1 min 53.4 secs	1 min 52.6 secs

L. Chiron	P.Walker	L. Rosier	E. De Graffenried
Maserati	E.R.A	Lago Talbot	Maserati
1 min 56.6 secs	1 min 56.6 secs	1 min 56 secs	1 min 55.8 secs

P. Etancelin	F.R.Gerard	L. Johnson
Lago Talbot	E.R.A	E.R.A
1 min 57.8 secs	1 min 57.4 secs	1 min 57.4 secs

D. Murray	G. Crossley	A. Hampshire	T.C.Harrison
Maserati	Alta	Maserati	E.R.A
2 min 05.6 secs	2 min 02.6 secs	2 min01.0 secs	1 min 58.4 secs

J. Claes	J.Fry	J.Kelly
Lago Talbot	Maserati	Alta
2 min 08.8 secs	2 min 07.0 secs	2 min 06.2 secs

The start of the Grand Prix d'Europe at Silverstone in 1950.

The race consisted of 70 laps over the 202.23 mile circuit and, from the fall of the flag, the four Alfa Romeos led the field in their grid order. Behind them, Bira lay fifth in front of three Lago Talbots. Disappointingly, mechanical problems forced the two new and sleek E Type E.R.A.s of Peter Walker and Leslie Johnson to become early retirements and after 5 laps the order was Giuseppe Farina, Juan Fangio, Luigi Fagioli and Reg Parnell. Farina sat

Bob Gerard in his E.R.A. R.14.B during the British Grand Prix.

Giuseppe Farina winning the 1950 British Grand Prix in his 158 Alfa Romeo.

at arms' length from his steering wheel, looking deceptively relaxed, while he and Fangio constantly exchanged the lead, giving the crowd of 150 000 something to get excited about. As the race progressed Prince Bira's Maserati stopped on Hanger Straight with fuel starvation, and the front of Parnell's Alfa was dented by a collision with a hare. The four Alfas refuelled in good order, each taking between 25 and 30 seconds to complete the operation and thereafter continued to command the race. Fagioli and Parnell followed the leading pair, comfortably ahead of the Lago Talbots of Yves Giraud-Cabantous and Louis Rosier. Then Fangio's car slid on a patch of oil at Stowe and consequently hit a straw bale. He retired two laps later with a broken connecting rod, but Farina's lead was such that he was able to slow down to enable Fagioli to finish within three seconds of him, while Parnell came home third, nearly a minute behind. Giraud-Cabantous, Rosier, Gerard, Cuth Harrison, and Philippe Etancelin occupied the next six places while Joe Kelly, in his sleek but underpowered Alta finished unclassified 13 laps behind. Farina's average speed for the race was 90.95mph. Bob Gerard was awarded the Fred Craner Memorial Trophy as the first British driver to finish in a British car. There were complaints after the race about the congested roads around Silverstone and also about the poor state of the essential amenities.

The result

1. G. Farina Alfa Romeo 2 hr. 13 mins 23.6 secs
2. L. Fagioli Alfa Romeo 2 hr. 13 mins 26.2 secs
3. R. Parnell Alfa Romeo 2 hr. 14 min 15.6 secs
4. Y. Giraud-Cabantous Lago Talbot 2 laps behind
5. L. Rosier Lago Talbot
6. F. R. Gerard E.R.A. 3 laps behind
7. T. C. Harrison E.R.A.
8. P. Etancelin Lago Talbot 5 laps behind
9. D. Hampshire Maserati 6 laps behind
10. J. G. Fry/ B. Shawe-Taylor Maserati
11. J. Claes Lago Talbot

J. Kelly Alta Unclassified and 13 laps behind.

Retirements: L. Johnson E.R.A. on lap 2 with a failed supercharger, P. Walker/A. Rolt E.R.A. on lap 5 with gearbox trouble, E. Martin Lago Talbot on lap 10 with low oil pressure, L. Chiron Maserati on lap 24 with clutch trouble.

The fastest lap was recorded by G. Farina on lap 2 at 94.02mph.

The Monaco Grand Prix. Monte Carlo: May 21

There were four Alfa Romeos at Monaco for Giuseppe Farina, Juan Fangio and Luigi Fagioli and Fangio gained pole position with Farina and Froilan Gonzales' 4CLT Maserati claiming the remaining two places on the front row of the grid. Fagioli was on the second row having been beaten by 0.1 sec in practice by Etancelin's Lago Talbot, and Luigi Villoresi and Alberto Ascari were sixth and seventh fastest in works 1.5 litre supercharged V12 Ferrari 125s. Maurice Trintignant and Robert Manzon were eleventh and thirteenth in their little Simca-Gordinis. Fangio overtook Farina to take the lead on the first lap and Farina was then overtaken first by Gonzales and then by Villoresi, who then proceeded to overtake Gonzales as well. Then disaster struck as Farina spun near the harbour wall on the spray from the sea and his car collected Gonzales, Fagioli, Louis Rosier, Trintignant, Franco Rol (Maserati), Toulo de Gaffenried (Maserati), Robert Manzon (Simca-Gordini), Cuth Harrison (E.R.A.), and Harry Schell (Cooper-J.A.P.). All these cars were too damaged to continue and, in a sadly depleted field, Fangio won the race at 61.33mph, one lap ahead of

Ascari with Louis Chiron's Maserati taking third place a further lap behind. Bob Gerard whose E.R.A. had been 16th in practice finished in sixth place 6 laps behind. Fangio also set the fastest lap of the race at 64.09mph.

The Swiss Grand Prix. Berne: June 4

The Alfa Romeos of Juan Fangio, Giuseppe Farina and Luigi Fagioli occupied the front row of the Swiss Grand Prix which was held on the Bremgarten circuit at Berne. Luigi Villoresi and Alberto Ascari in 1.5 litre supercharged V12 Tipo 125 Ferraris were immediately behind then. Villoresi's Ferrari had a new lengthened chassis to improve its road holding and Ascari's a five speed gearbox. There were no British cars or drivers and the

Alberto Ascari driving the Tipo 125 V12 1.5 litre two stage supercharged Ferrari in the 1950 Swiss Grand Prix at Berne.

two Lago Talbots of Philippe Etancelin and Yves Giraud-Cabantous and the Maserati of Prince Bira formed the third row. The three Alfas followed by the two Ferraris set the early pattern of the race, but Ascari had displaced Fagioli before retiring on lap three. Villoresi also got ahead of Fagioli's Alfa Romeo before he too retired on lap 9. On lap 33 Fangio had to drop out from second place with valve trouble but the race went to the two Alfas of Farina and Fagioli followed by Louis Rosier in his faithful Lago Talbot and Bira's 4CLT Maserati. Farina's winning speed was 92.7mph.

Farina also made the fastest lap of the race at 100.78mph.

The Belgian Grand Prix. Spa: June 18

Alfa Romeos filled the front row of the starting grid again at Spa with Giuseppe Farina and Juan Fangio posting almost identical times, while Luigi Fagioli was a full four seconds slower. The Ferraris of Luigi Villoresi and Alberto Ascari were 5th and 8th in practice, being split by the Lago Talbots of Raymond Sommer and Philippe Etancelin. Villoresi again drove the 1.5 litre supercharged V12 125 Ferrari while Ascari had the new 3.3 litre unsupercharged V12 Tipo 375 car. The main opposition to the Italian cars consisted of no less than seven 4.5 litre Lago Talbots. It took a whole lap for Fagioli to displace Villoresi's Ferrari and to establish the familiar formation of the "three Fs," Fangio being the leader on this occasion. Then Raymond Sommer passed all three of them with his Lago Talbot as the supercharged cars were forced to come into the pits to refuel. Sadly the Frenchman's brave effort came to an end when he retired with a blown engine on lap 20, when he was still to be overtaken by the third Alfa Romeo. Eventually the Alfas and Ferraris all had to stop again for fuel and tyres and in the end it was Louis Rosier's Lago Talbot that finished third, behind Fangio and Fagioli and in front of Farina who had been delayed with falling oil pressure. The Ferraris of Ascari and Villoresi were fifth and sixth.

Fangio's winning speed was 110.048mph and the fastest lap was set by Farina at 115.40mph.

The French Grand Prix. Rheims: July 2

In a later age any race that was dominated by one team might have been considered dull and processional but such was not the case in 1950. Even in the absence of Ferrari and with their opponents proving to be fragile, the magnificent Alfa Romeos didn't fail to stir the crowd's enthusiasm at Rheims. It was a 64 lap race of 310.78 miles and Giuseppe Farina, Juan Fangio and Luigi Fagioli inevitably drew away from the rest from the start. Fangio and Fagioli secured the first two places but Farina, having led initially, was only classified seventh, nine laps behind, after stopping with a problem with his fuel pump. Peter Whitehead finished third in his privately entered 1.5 litre Ferrari but the retirements outnumbered the finishers and included the privately entered 4CLT Maseratis of David Hampshire and Reg Parnell. Fangio was a worthy victor, having established the fastest lap of the race at 112.35mph and winning at an average speed of 104.84mph.

The Italian Grand Prix. Monza: September 3

The Alfa Romeos of Fangio and Farina closely followed by the Ferraris of Albert Ascari and Froilan Gonzales during the Italian Grand Prix.

As always, the Grand Prix at Monza was the race that the Italian teams most wanted to win. Ferrari brought along 4.5 litre cars for Alberto Ascari and Dorino Serafini and a 3.3 litre

model for Luigi Villoresi. The Alfa Romeo trio were joined by Consalvo Senesi and Piero Taruffi, and Juan Fangio and Giuseppe Farina had the improved 159 models. It was a vitally important race for them as they both had an equal number of Championship points and the outcome would determine which would become the first World Champion. Ascari was second to Fangio in practice and Farina and Sanesi completed the front row of the starting grid. At the start Farina held on to a narrow lead from Ascari who pressed him hard and snatched it from him briefly on lap 14. Then both Ascari and Fangio retired with major mechanical woes, but Fangio was given Taruffi's Alfa Romeo, and Ascari took over Serafini's Ferrari which had been lying in sixth place. Fangio retired for a second time on lap 35 but Ascari overtook Fagioli when his Alfa had to stop for fuel. The result was that the Ferrari driven by both Serafini and Ascari finished second to Farina while Fagioli came third. The Lago Talbots of Louis Rosier and Philippe Etancelin finished fourth and fifth. Villoresi, having spun on a patch of oil, was eliminated from the race as a result of the crash. Ascari had shown that the 4.5 litre Ferrari could match the pace of the 159 Alfa Romeo while, in addition, it had the crucial advantage of being able to cover more laps before having to stop to refuel.

Farina's winning speed was 109.70mph while Fangio established the fastest lap at 117.44mph.

The World Championship

Juan Fangio had finished the Season strongly but Guiseppe Farina emerged as the first World Champion with 30 points while Juan Fangio had 27. The order after this was Luigi Fagioli 24, Louis Rosier 13, Alberto Ascari 11. Reg Parnell came 9th with the 4 points he earned at Silverstone.

NON CHAMPIONSHIP EVENTS
Goodwood Easter Monday

During practice before the Easter Monday meeting at Goodwood in 1950 Reg Parnell demonstrated the potential danger of straw bales when his foot slipped in changing down to enter Lavant corner, causing his 4CLT Maserati to come off the circuit and to ram into them. Heat from his exhaust ignited the straw but fortunately Parnell had already jumped out and the fire was soon extinguished.

There was little chance of a similar problem on race day as driving rain resulted in sodden straw. The latest E Type E.R.A. of Peter Walker was a non starter, which was a pity although the car never performed as well as it looked.

I always associate rain with Goodwood in the 1950s and during the Richmond Trophy Race a downpour determined the result. I was standing out in the open with my brothers John and David at the end of the Lavant straight, and watched the cars literally streaming past at the end of the first lap. The press had conferred the title 'King of Goodwood' upon Reg Parnell the previous year and he was confidently expected to win the race, but Baron Toulo de Graffenried and Prince Bira also had the latest San Remo 4CLT Maseratis and, in addition, there was the usual assortment of E.R.A.s, two of which were driven by Brian Shaw Taylor and Cuth Harrison. Bira's Maserati was of course painted in his nation's colours of blue and yellow, and de Graffenried's identical car was in the Swiss colours of red and white. It also had yellow wheels which made it easy to distinguish from Parnell's car, in spite of the conditions.

It was Harrison who led momentarily at the start of the race but he was soon overtaken by the three Maseratis of Bira, de Graffenried and Parnell. Parnell had made a poor start but the two leading drivers, wearing goggles, found that the rain all but obscured their vision whereas Parnell, with a visor, had a distinct advantage. First Bira eased back and dropped

Reg Parnell winning the Richmond Trophy Race at Goodwood on Easter Monday in his 4CLT Maserati, followed by Baron Toulo de Graffenried.

out of contention and then de Graffenried found it impossible to hold Parnell off any longer. With only four cars left in the 11 lap race Parnell swept past into the lead on the eighth lap and de Graffenried took the opportunity to wipe his goggles with his hand. The order after the Maseratis was Brian Shaw Taylor and Graham Whitehead, both driving E.R.A.s.

The *Daily Express* Trophy Race. Silverstone: August 16

The *Daily Express* International Trophy Race at Silverstone was intended to show case the new 16 cylinder B.R.M. in its first race and I still have my copy of 'B.R.M. Ambassador for Britain' which the *Daily Express* had produced to herald its arrival. I listened intently to

Yves Giraud-Cabantous at speed in his Lago Talbot during the International Trophy Race at Silverstone on August 26th.

Raymond Baxter's description of the start of the second heat. A sole B.R.M. lined up at the back of the grid having arrived too late for the practice and when the flag fell the car, with Raymond Sommer at the wheel, moved only inches as its transmission failed. After countless practice starts on the Folkingham Airfield in Lincolnshire it chose to break then!

Juan Fangio crossing the line to win Heat 2 of the International Trophy Race in his Alfa Romeo.

Both the 15 lap heats went to the works 158 Alfas Romeos. Heat One being led from start to finish by Giuseppe Farina while heat two was in the gift of Juan Fangio. In the 35 lap

B G Apps

final the two Alfas were unchallenged, with Fangio appearing to make a race of it with his team mate while the result was never in doubt.

Goodwood: September 30

Following its debacle at Silverstone a B.R.M. was entered for the September meeting at Goodwood to be driven by Reg Parnell. It rained throughout the races for the 5 lap Woodcote Cup and the 12 lap Goodwood Trophy. In the first of these short sprints Reg, starting cautiously, was initially led by Toulo de Graffenried's Maserati and Peter

Reg Parnell winning the Goodwood Trophy Race with the V16 B.R.M. still in its original form and colour on September 30 1950.

Whitehead's E.R.A., but he soon got into his stride and, overtaking them, led for the rest of the race, although Prince Bira's 4CLT Maserati closed up to him towards the end. Starting from the second row of the grid for the Goodwood Trophy Race, Parnell took the lead from Bira early on the first lap. Never getting into top gear, he held off Bira, who closed up on the corners, by powering away on the straights. It was a mildly encouraging result but the B.R.M. had yet to be tested in a full length Grand Prix against the Alfa Romeos and Ferraris in fine conditions when its engine could be fully extended.

Peter Walker's V16 B.R.M. during the Spanish Grand Prix.

The Spanish Grand Prix: October 29

The Spanish Grand Prix at Pena Rhin Barcelona was a non Championship Race but offered competition from the works Ferraris in genuinely Grand Prix conditions. Two B.R.M.s were entered for Reg Parnell and Peter Walker to drive. Walker's car stalled on the starting line but Parnell, having almost stalled his engine too, came through from the back of the field, passing seventeen cars on the first lap to catch up with the

Alberto Ascari winning the
Spanish Grand Prix in his 4.5
litre Ferrari.

third Ferrari. Sadly, his race was over on lap 2 with a sheared drive in his supercharger!
Walker was fifth by lap 33 but then he too was forced to retire with a gearbox failure. The
press was unforgiving but I thought it was a brave effort this early in the car's development.

The Monte Carlo Rally

A Jowett Javelin being
craned aboard the *Dinard* at
Folkestone during the 1950
Monte Carlo Rally.

Most of the cars competing in the 1950 Monte Carlo Rally had special equipment
to help them cope with the challenging conditions. Many had spot lights and
search lights, additional spare wheels, chains, and spades. Some had map tables
for the passengers, padded headrests and kilometre speedometers. One had
an opening on its scuttle through which hot air from the engine was directed
on to the windscreen and another even had an adaptation inside the car to
power an electric razor!

The first to start from Glasgow was C. F. Bartlett in a bright red Vauxhall and, striving to keep up with him and all the other competitors, was Richard Dimbleby in an Allard Coupe. *Motor Sport* reported that the Glasgow contingent drove through London at a 'rousing speed' without any intervention from the police. Heavy and continuous snow was encountered on the road to Monte Carlo and, of the 282 cars that set out from Glasgow, Lisbon, Stockholm, Oslo, Florence and Monte Carlo only 182 actually completed the 2000 mile journey, the others having fallen by the way side for a variety of reasons. The competitors arrived at Monaco in torrential rain, the first British car to arrive being the Imhof/Hutchison Allard in spite of crashing into a telegraph pole on route! A Standard Vanguard was the next to finish. In the end the winner was a 3.5 litre Hotchkiss driven by Marcel Becquart and H. Secret, but only one mark behind in second place was the Humber Super Snipe of Gatsonides and Barendregt. A similar Hotchkiss 686 had won the Rally in 1949 but, in spite of its success, production of the model ceased in 1950. Only five cars had qualified for the important acceleration, reversing and braking test, the other three being French Simcas. *Motor Sport* described the Rally as 'quite the finest non racing event held' and praised the B.B.C.'s coverage by Raymond Baxter. The Concours de Confort was won by W.M. Couper's magnificent Park Ward bodied Rolls Royce Silver Wraith in spite of it having hit a lorry near Valence.

The Mille Miglia

There were 383 starters for the 17th 1000 mile Brescia to Brescia road race for sports and touring cars which, in 1950, was run in treacherous conditons. Sixteen Ferraris were entered for the race and the four Marzotto brothers were amongst their drivers. Alberto Ascari and

Alberto Ascari's 166MM Ferrari during the 1950 Mille Miglia.

Giuseppe Villoresi had new works 3 litre cars while Juan Fangio and Franco Rol drove 2.5 litre Alfa Romeos. Felice Bonetto's Alfa was powered by a 4.5 litre pre-war Grand Prix engine and Consalvo Sanesi was given an experimental 3 litre Alfa for the race. There were several XK120 Jaguars in the hands of Clemente Biondetti, who had won the event four times before, Johnson, Wisdom, Hume, Haines, Haller, Ideb and Gaboardi. Healey Silverstones were well represented by Wood and Monkhouse, Richards and Lord, and Donald Healey himself, and there was a pre-war Aston Martin driven by Stapleton and Ruffo. Fog and torrential rain added to the danger and there was a high number of accidents as the cars raced on the public roads through towns and cities and took on the rugged country roads in between them. Villoresi led the earlier stages of the race and Leslie Johnson ran courageously in fifth place, but both Villoresi and Ascari retired with transmission problems after Villoresi had averaged 92mph for more than one-third of the race. The ultimate winner was the V12 2.340cc Ferrari of Giannini Marzotto and Marco Crosara which maintained an average speed of 76.57mph. Serafini/Zari came second in a 3.3 litre Ferrari, Fangio third, and Bracco fourth in a 2 litre Ferrari. The Johnson/Lee Jaguar finished in fifth place, Cortese's 2 litre Frazer Nash Le Mans was sixth and Biondetti's XK120 Jaguar eighth. Prince Lanza's Cisitalia crashed over the side of an embankment, and Peter Monkhouse was fatally injured when his Healey Silverstone left the road at the same point.

Le Mans

The field of the famous 24 Hour Race at Le Mans was led away from the start by Raymond Sommer's Ferrari and it set the pace before eventually retiring with transmission trouble. The race then went to Louis Rosier and his son Jean-Claude who drove a 4.5 litre Talbot. Their car was a thinly veiled Grand Prix Lago Talbot with a 2-seater sports car body and motorcycle type mudguards and after, leading for all but the first two laps of the race they won at an average speed of 89.73mph. Another Talbot came second, driven by Pierre

The Nash-Healey of Hamilton/ Rolt with which they finished in fourth place at Le Mans in 1950.

The Hall/Clark Bentley which finished in eighth place at Le Mans.

Meyrat and Guy Mairesse. Having enjoyed watching new J2 Allards being tested on the road round Clapham Common, I was thrilled that Sydney Allard and Tom Cole came third in one of these cars, powered by a 5.4 litre Cadillac engine. Tony Rolt and Duncan Hamilton finished fourth in a 3.8 litre Nash-Healey, and a 2.5 litre DB1 Aston Martin driven by George

The Briggs Cunningham/Phil Walters Cadillac engined Cunningham during the 1950 Le Mans 24 Hour Race.

Abecassis and Lance Macklin was fifth. This was David Brown's second Le Mans, and a DB2 driven by Brackenbury and Parnell finished in sixth place. A second works DB2, driven by Fairman/Thompson, retired after three hours. Jack Fairman had crashed the car they were to have raced at Brionne in Normandy while driving it down to Le Mans on the public roads so they were forced to drive a spare car in the race instead! Other British entries included three of the new Jaguar XK120s, this being the first assault of William Lyons and Jaguar on Le Mans. The car driven by Clark/Haines finished 12th and that of Whitehead/Marshall 20th. The Johnson/Hadley Jaguar retired near the end but had been running in seventh place. Two 4.5 litre Bentleys finished 8th and 14th, the second one having already completed 125,000 miles before the race! A 1.2 litre M.G. finished in 18th place, a Jowett Jupiter 16th and two Frazer Nash cars 9th and 20th. The event also witnessed Briggs Cunningham's first attempt at Le Mans. His standard looking 5.4 litre Cadillac saloon finished 10th while he himself came 11th in a Cadillac which, boasting a streamlined Cunningham body, was dubbed 'Le Monstre'. He would be back.

The Index of Performance Cup was awarded jointly to the Abecassis/Macklin Aston Martin and the Montremy/Hemand Monople. The 5 to 8 litre Class was won by the Allard/Cole Allard and the 2 to 3 litre Class by the Abecassis/Macklin Aston Martin.

1951
Juan Fangio establishes his mastery

ENZO FERRARI HAD demonstrated in the Italian Grand Prix at Monza that Alfa Romeo could no longer expect to have things all its own way in Formula 1 and, in the absence of the Alfa Romeo team, the 4.5 litre Ferraris had taken the first three places in the non Championship Spanish Grand Prix at Barcelona on October 29.

In 1951 the more powerful 159 Alfa Romeos could manage only one and a half miles to the gallon. Measures to increase their fuel capacity gave the cars a more swollen appearance without preventing them from having to make two stops to refuel during each race. The 4.5 litre Ferraris were now equipped with 24 plug heads and a newcomer in 1951 was the 4.5 litre OSCA built by the Maserati brothers. It had a 4CLT Maserati chassis and was driven by Prince Bira. A supporting role was played by private entrants with Lago Talbots and there were also Simca-Gordinis, and the H.W.M.s driven by John Heath, George Abecassis, Stirling Moss and others.

THE WORLD CHAMPIONSHIP SEASON
The Swiss Grand Prix. Berne: May 27

The 4.5 litre Ferraris were driven again at Berne by Alberto Ascari, Luigi Villoresi and Piero Taruffi while the 159 Alfa Romeos, with their enlarged fuel tanks, were in the hands of Juan Fangio, Giuseppe Farina, Consalvo Sanesi and Toulo de Graffenried. Rudi Fischer drove a privately entered 2.5 litre unsupercharged Ferrari while Peter Whitehead had his 1.5 supercharged Tipo 125. During the first practice day only one Alfa Romeo was used, its racing numbers being changed for each of the drivers in turn. Farina tried a crash helmet with a greatly extended

Juan Manuel Fangio.

visor but discarded it when it threatened to blow his head off at speed! Three mechanics were assigned to each of the Alfa Romeos, and anti-splash shields were adopted on both of the works Italian teams for the first time, with good cause because heavy rain would dominate the race. Italian cars filled the first ten places on the starting grid with Fangio, Farina and Villoresi occupying the front row. Stirling Moss and George Abecassis were 14th and 20th in their H.W.M.s while Froilan Gonzales drove a 1950 2-seater Lago

Talbot to 13th place on the grid. Worried about the prospect of enforced pit stops the Alfa drivers had their fuel tanks topped up on the starting grid immediately before the race. In driving rain the Alfa Romeos took an immediate lead and after five laps the order was Fangio, Farina, Villoresi, Sanesi and de Graffenried. Ascari was still recovering from the burns he had sustained in a race in Geneva but Taruffi forced his way up to third place after Villoresi had crashed as a result of being blinded by spray from the car in front of him. Fangio maintained his lead in spite of his first pit stop but Taruffi put his Ferrari ahead of Farina to take second place, splitting the Alfa Romeos. Stirling Moss was robbed of seventh place when the engine of his 2 litre H.W.M. cut out, allowing Chiron to cross the line ahead of him in his Maserati. Gonzales had retired on lap 10 with low oil pressure. The Alfa Romeos of Farina, Sanesi, and de Graffenried were third, fourth and fifth, while Ascari's Ferrari followed them in sixth place.

Fangio won the race at an average speed of 89.108mph and set the fastest lap of the race at 95.178mph.

The Belgian Grand Prix. Spa: June 17

It had become clear at Spa that the Alfa Romeos and Ferraris were very evenly matched and so there was every prospect of it being a close race. On a brilliant June afternoon the Alfa Romeo team of Juan Fangio, Giuseppe Farina and Conslavo Sanesi was split by the Ferraris of Luigi Villoresi, Alberto Ascari and Piero Taruffi who were third, fourth and fifth on the starting grid.

Ascari jumped the start while Sanesi stalled his engine and when the field settled down it was Villoresi who led, followed by Farina, Ascari, Fangio and Taruffi. Then Farina overtook Villoresi and started to draw away from the rest until Fangio established the fastest lap of the race in the course of a charge which brought him right up to his team mate. Much swapping of positions took place until Fangio was firmly ahead of Farina and the Ferraris had begun to drop back. Sanesi retired with a holed radiator, and Fangio was held at the pits by a wheel which was stuck fast to its hub. Eventually the tyre had to be removed from its rim and it was over 14 minutes before Fangio could return to the race. The result was a win for Farina at 114.25mph with the second and third places going to the Ferraris of Ascari and Villoresi. Lago Talbots filled the next five places.

The fastest lap of the race was recorded by Fangio at 120.509mph.

The French Grand Prix. Rheims: July 1

Reg Parnell arrived in Rheims to drive Tony Vandervell's 4.5 litre Thin Wall Special Ferrari and the Alfa Romeo/Ferrari dual was on again for the Grand Prix d'Europe. The race was run over 77 laps of the 4.86 mile circuit and the Argentinian Froilan Gonzales was to drive a works Ferrari. Juan Fangio (Alfa Romeo), Giuseppe Farina (Alfa Romeo) and Alberto Ascari (Ferrari) lined up at the front in that order, with Luigi Villoresi (Ferrari) and Consalvo Sanesi (Alfa Romeo) immediately behind them. Parnell was ninth in practice with four Lago Talbots behind him and two more in front. Both Villoresi and Sanesi crept forward immediately before the start but it was Ascari who established an initial lead from Farina. Then Ascari was delayed at his pit with brake problems and Farina led while Luigi Fagioli temporarily left the road. Fangio lost several minutes in the pits and then took over Fagioli's Alfa Romeo. The situation then was that Farina led, followed by Gonzales, Villoresi, Fangio and Parnell in the green Thin Wall Special. Fangio proceeded to establish a new lap record of 118.29mph in recovering to third position and Ascari took over Gonzales' car when it was brought in for fuel. Farina's Alfa threw a tread and so lost over three minutes in the pits and the order became Ascari, Fangio, Farina, Villoresi and Parnell. Yet there were more twists and turns of fate to come and Ascari had to pit for adjustments to be made to his brakes. So the Fagioli/Fangio Alfa Romeo won the race at 110.972mph from the Gonzales/ Ascari Ferrari. Villoresi was third and Parnell fourth.

The British Grand Prix. Silverstone: July 14

A crowd of only 50,000 came to watch the two B.R.M.s of Reg Parnell and Peter Walker start from the back row of the grid at Silverstone as, having arrived at 7 00 a.m on the race day, they were too late for the official practice. Significantly Froilan Gonzales had been fastest in practice with the 4.5 litre Ferrari, and the front row was completed by Juan Fangio and Giuseppe Farina in Alfa Romeos and Alberto Ascari in the second Ferrari. Luigi Villoresi (Ferrari), Consalvo Sanesi (Alfa Romeo) and Felice Bonetto (Alfa Romeo) occupied the second row so that another close contest between the two Italian teams was assured.

The Starting Grid

A. Ascari	G. Farina	J.M Fangio	J.F Gonzales
Ferrari	Alfa Romeo	Alfa Romeo	Ferrari
1 min 45.4 secs	1 min 45.0 secs	1 min 44.4 secs	1 min 43.4 secs

	F. Bonetto	C. Sanesi	L. Villoresi	
	Alfa Romeo	Alfa Romeo	Ferrari	
	1 min 52.0 secs	1 min 50.2 secs	1 min 45.8 secs	

D. Hamilton	F.R. Gerard	L. Rosier	P. Whitehead
Lago Talbot	E.R.A	Lago Talbot	Ferrari
1 min 57.2 secs	1 min 57 secs	1 min 56 secs	1 min 54.6 secs

	J. Claes	L. Chiron	B. Shawe-Taylor	
	Lago Talbot	Lago Talbot	E.R.A	
	2 min 05.8 secs	2 min 00.2 secs	1 min 58.2 secs	

J. Kelly	J. James	J. Fotheringham-Parker	D. Murray
Alta	Maserati	Maserati	Maserati
2 min 18.4 secs	2 mins 17.0secs	2 mins 13.2 secs	2 mins 6.0 secs

	R. Parnell	P. Walker	
	B.R.M	B.R.M.	

No times

Felice Bonetto made a magnificent start to lead the race initially and he was closely followed by Froilan Gonzales and Giuseppe Farina. By the time that Gonzales had succeeded in overtaking the flying Italian Juan Fangio had come through from 5th place to set off after his fellow Argentinian. The B.R.M. drivers were forced to ease back after an initial surge to avoid the back markers and the race became a battle royal between Gonzales and Fangio. Fangio took the lead on lap 10 but twenty-eight laps later Gonzales regained it getting ahead of him again, never having been far behind. Farina was lying third behind his team mate and ahead of Ascari. None of the Alfa Romeos, apart from Bonetto's car, was equipped with side tanks and so they had to come into the pits to refuel, handing to the Ferraris their expected advantage. Ascari retired with gearbox trouble on lap 56 and Farina abandoned the race with a failed clutch on lap 76. Gonzales held off his fellow countryman to win at a speed of 96.11mph, Fangio having to settle for second place after a spirited drive,

Reg Parnell's B.R.M. being lapped by Alberto Ascari's Ferrari during the 1951 British Grand Prix.

Signed painting of Juan Fangio driving the 159 Alfa Romeo in the British Grand Prix.

and Villoresi's Ferrari was third. In a memorable race the Alfa Romeos had been vanquished at last by a Ferrari. The two B.R.M.s finished in fifth and seventh places, Parnell and Walker being separated by Sanesi's Alfa Romeo. It could have been seen as an encouraging

Froilan Gonzales winning the British Grand Prix in his 4.5 litre Ferrari.

performance, bearing in mind that the two drivers had been instructed to limit their revs and both suffered severe burns from their exhausts. Brian Shawe-Taylor and Bob Gerard were 8th and 11th in their E.R.A.s and Hamilton 12th in his Lago Talbot.

Results

1. J.F. Gonzales Ferrari 2 hr. 42 mins 18 secs
2. J.M. Fangio Alfa Romeo 2 hr. 43 mins 9.2 secs
3. L. Villoresi Ferrari 2 laps behind.
4. F. Bonetto Alfa Romeo 3 laps behind.
5. R. Parnell B.R.M. 5 laps behind.
6. C. Sanesi Alfa Romeo 6 laps behind.
7. P. Walker B.R.M.
8. B. Shawe-Taylor E.R.A.
9. P. Whitehead Ferrari 7 laps behind
10. L. Rosier Lago Talbot
11. F. R. Gerard E.R.A. 8 laps behind.
12. D. Hamilton Lago Talbot
13. J. Claes Lago Talbot 10 laps behind.

Retirements: J. James Maserati on lap 23 with damaged radiator, L. Chiron Lago Talbot on lap 41 with brake failure, D. Murray Maserati on lap 45 with a broken valve spring, J. Fotheringham-Parker Maserati on lap 46 with broken oil pipe, A. Ascari Ferrari on lap 56 with gearbox trouble, G. Farina Alfa Romeo on lap 76 with clutch trouble.

Fastest lap was set by Farina at 99.99mph.

Stirling Moss winning the 500cc Race in his Kieft-Norton during the British Grand Prix meeting at Sliverstone.

The German Grand Prix. Nurburgring: July 29

The pattern of Formula 1 in 1951 was firmly established when the teams arrived at the Nurburgring for the German Grand Prix. It was the first Formula 1 Grand Prix to be held on the Nurburgring since the war and the Ferraris of Alberto Ascari and Froilan Gonzales shared the front row of the grid with the Alfa Romeos of Juan Fangio and Giuseppe Farina. Only 4.8 seconds separating the practice times of the first four cars on the 14 mile circuit. A third Alfa Romeo was driven by Paul Pietsch who was familiar with the Nurburgring but he was slower than Ferraris of Luigi Villoresi and Piero Taruffi. Duncan Hamilton was 20th in his Lago Talbot.

After leading initially, Farina was overtaken by Fangio, Ascari and Gonzales on the first of the 20 laps. Ascari overtook Fangio on lap 5 and then all the Alfas dropped out of contention when they stopped to refuel. Farina retired with gearbox problems on lap 8 but Fangio set about making up for lost time. He recovered the lead when the Ferraris had their pit stops but then had to stop for a second time on lap 14. This allowed Ascari to resume the lead which he retained to the end. Fangio was the sole survivor of the Alfa drivers, Pietsch having crashed out on lap 12. Gonzales came home third, after Ascari and Fangio, to be followed by Villoresi, Taruffi and Rudi Fischer, all of whom were driving Ferraris. Duncan Hamilton had retired with low oil pressure on lap 12.

Ascari's average speed for the race was 83.76mph and the fastest lap was recorded by Fangio at 85.69mph.

The Italian Grand Prix. Monza: September 16

The Italian Grand Prix at Monza offered the V16 B.R.M. its last chance to shine in a World Championship event but it all went disastrously wrong. Peter Walker had not recovered from his Silverstone burns and the R.A.C. refused to allow test driver Ken Richardson to drive the second car in his place. Richardson had bent the steering arm of his car when he left the circuit at some speed in practice and this was repaired by Alfa Romeo after being approached on B.R.M.'s behalf by Count Johnny Lurani. Hans Stuck came forward as a second substitute to partner Reg Parnell but engine failures and gear box problems caused both cars to be withdrawn from the race. The two cars had gained 7th and 9th places on the starting grid and, while they were undoubtedly fragile and still at an early stage of

Alberto Ascari winning the
1951 Italian Grand Prix.

development, they impressed everyone both with their speed on the straights and, of course, by the distinctive sound of their engines.

The field was left open to the Italians, the Alfa Romeos of Juan Fangio and Giuseppe Farina being first and second in practice. The brand new 4.5 Ferraris of Alberto Ascari and Froilan Gonzales, which had their headrests moulded into their tails, were third and fourth. Luigi Villoresi (Ferrari), Piero Taruffi (Ferrari), Felice Bonetto (Alfa Romeo) and Toulo de Graffenried in an earlier 159 Alfa Romeo, completed the line up of the two teams in that order. Franco Rol was 18th in the 4.5 litre OSCA.

At the start of the race Ascari led from Fangio, Farina and Gonzales and after Fangio had snatched the lead he was forced to pull into his pit with a blown tyre. Troubles were heaped on Alfa Romeo when Farina was forced to stop on lap 7 with a burst engine. Thereafter Ascari's lead was unchallenged but Fangio recovered to run in third place behind the Ferraris of Ascari and Gonzales. Farina took over Bonetto's Alfa Romeo when it stopped for fuel. Fangio retired on lap 40 when his engine cut out for the last time, but Farina was now in third place and gaining on Gonzales. After losing more time in the pits Farina resumed his pursuit and once more began to reduce the deficit. Then on lap 70 he came into the pits out of fuel and discovered that the tank of this older Alfa which he had inherited from Bonetto had split. He struggled on until the end, continuing to leak fuel and unable to do anything about the two Ferraris ahead of him. Ascari was left to win the race at a speed of 115.523mph followed by Gonzales, Bonetto/ Farina, Villoresi, and Taruffi. It was Ferrari's greatest success, not only winning the race but having four cars in the first five places. The lone OSCA finished in ninth place thirteen laps behind the winner.

The fastest lap was established by Farina at 121.488mph.

The Spanish Grand Prix. Barcelona: October 28

A crowd of 250 000 came to watch the last race of the season, knowing that its outcome would decide who would be the World Champion as Alberto Ascari and Juan Fangio were only separated by 2 points. B.R.M. stayed away, the cars having been held at Monza for high speed tests conducted by Fangio, Stirling Moss and others. Predictably, Alfa Romeos and Ferraris filled the first two rows of the starting grid. Ascari secured pole position with Fangio alongside him just 1.5 seconds slower, while Froilan Gonzales and Giuseppe Farina completed the front row Luigi Villoresi (Ferrari), Toulo de Graffenried (Alfa Romeo) and Piero Taruffi (Ferrari) shared the second row while Felice Bonetto (Alfa Romeo) was on the third row with the three Simca-Gordinis of Robert Manzon, Andre Simon and Maurice Trintignant. Behind these were six Lago Talbots, two 4CLT Maseratis and Bira's 4.5 litre OSCA.

Ascari snatched an early lead at the start of the race and at the end of the first lap he was followed by Farina, Fangio, Bonetto, Villoresi and Gonzales. However by lap 4 Fangio had moved ahead to take the lead after Ascari's near side rear tyre was shredded, and he proceeded to consolidate his position. Taruffi and Villoresi also had to stop with thrown treads as Enzo Ferrari had made the disastrous error of using smaller diameter wheels. Gonzales was similarly delayed and found himself separated from both Fangio and Farina by a significant margin. Ascari had to stop yet again for tyres but Gonzales was by now going well and he snatched second place from Farina when the Alfa came in for fuel. All the same it was Fangio's race and Fangio's first World Championship. He was followed across the line by Gonzales, Farina, Ascari, Bonetto and de Graffenried. It seemed that, tyre choices apart, Ferrari was just getting stronger and stronger, forcing Alfa Romeo to face up to the fact that the 1938 Alfetta had reached the end of its development. The question was, if the World Championship winning cars withdrew from racing in 1952, what would be the future of Formula 1?

Juan Fangio's 159 Alfa Romeo during the 1951 Spanish Grand Prix at Barcelona.

The World Championship

At the end of the 1951 Season Juan Fangio emerged as the World Champion with 31 points, Alberto Ascari had 25, Froilan Gonzales 24, Giuseppe Farina 19, Luigi Villoresi 15 and Piero Taruffi 10. Reg Parnell came 10th with 5 points.

NON CHAMPIONSHIP RACES
The *Daily Express* International Trophy Race. Silverstone: May 5

The *Daily Express* International Trophy Race at Silverstone proved to be yet another British event in which rain became the dominant feature. It also provided a rare opportunity for the British crowd to see the latest 159 Alfa Romeos in action. Four cars were to be driven by Juan Fangio, Giuseppe Farina, Felice Bonetto and Conslavo Sanesi in two heats and a final. It was disappointing that the Ferrari team was absent but Tony Vandervell, having given up on the B.R.M. project, had entered his twelve-month-old 4.5 litre Ferrari which he called the Thin Wall Special. Reg Parnell was to drive it and the crowd regarded it as a legitimate focus for its support. In the first heat Fangio led at the start from Bonetto and Parnell, the other two Alfas being reserved for the second heat. Behind the leaders came Brian Shawe-Taylor's E.R.A., Robert Manzon's Simca, David Murray's 4CLT Maserati and Louis Rosier's 4.5 litre Lago Talbot. For the first five laps Bonetto succeeded in holding Parnell off, allowing Fangio to build up a ten seconds lead. Then Parnell came through to second place and set about catching Fango. The green Ferrari was only 3 seconds behind at the end of the race. Farina and Sanesi were the stars of the second heat and having led throughout finished in that order with Bira's 4CLT Maserati and Gerard's E.R.A. in third and fourth places. Heavy rain threatened the final from the start and Parnell was in his element. He led the pack in the downpour followed by Duncan Hamilton's Lago Talbot and Peter Whitehead's E.R.A.

Reg Parnell overtaking Felice Bonetto's 159 Alfa Romeo in the 1950 4.5 litre Thin Wall Special during the First Heat of the International Trophy Race at Silverstone.

Stirling Moss winning the Production Car Race at Silverstone on May 5 in his XK120 Jaguar.

The track was awash and the rain caused the race to be abandoned after only six of the thirty-five laps. The result was not officially recognised as the race had been so short, but Fangio only managed third place and Farina ninth. Had the race continued it might have proved to be the first occasion when a Ferrari defeated the Alfa Romeos but as it was this would not happen until the epic dual between Fangio and Gonzales in the British Grand Prix at Silverstone.

The Festival of Britain Trophy Race. Goodwood: Whit Sunday

The Festival of Britain Trophy Race at Goodwood was run over two 7 lap heats and a final. The first heat was dominated by Reg Parnell in the 4.5 Thin Wall Special Ferrari. Competing against him were the 4CLT Maseratis of Baron de Graffenried, and David

The author's London Transport Bus ticket for the Festival of Britain which has somehow survived the changes and chances of life.

Murray, whose name would later be associated with the Ecurie Ecosse Jaguar team, Tony Rolt's E.R.A. engined ex Dick Seaman Delage, Duncan Hamilton's Lago Talbot, and the E.R.A.s of Bob Gerard, Brian Shaw-Taylor, Graham Whitehead and Claude Hamilton. At the end Parnell was 7 seconds ahead of de Graffenried and Shaw-Taylor finished third.

The star of the second heat was Giuseppe Farina but he was driving his own 4CLT Maserati and not a works Alfa Romeo. He had to pit his skill against the 4.5 litre OSCA of Prince Bira, the Maseratis of Harry Schell, David Hampshire and Kenneth McAlpine, and the pre-war 8C Alfa Romeo of Dennis Poore. Poore led at the start but was overtaken first by Bira and then by Farina. These finished first and second with Hampshire third.

The start of the Festival of Britain Trophy race at Goodwood on Whit Monday. From left to right: Reg Parnell (Thin Wall Special), Giuseppe Farina (4CLT Maserati), Baron Toulo de Graffenried (4CLT Maserati), Prince Bira (OSCA)

Giuseppe Farina with his 4CLT Maserati during the Festival of Britain Trophy Race.

Stirling Moss in his H.W.H.
at Goodwood in 1951.

In the final Parnell led convincingly at first but Farina reduced his lead forcing him to respond with a new lap record of 94.53mph. At the finish Parnell won the race with Farina by 10.8 seconds and Toulo de Gaffenried finished third in his 4CLT Maserati.

The Monte Carlo Rally

The weather for the 1951 Monte Carlo Rally was less extreme than in 1950 and only 54 of the 337 entrants failed to reach Monte Carlo. 111 failed to incur penalty points. 64 cars left from Glasgow, flagged away by the Lord Provost, for the four day journey to Monte Carlo and only one failed to reach Folkestone after driving through the night. Special equipment included headlamp wipers, while the drivers of a Hillman Minx had a two-way radio. The event was won for the fourth time by Jean Trevoux who drove a Delahaye with R. Crovetto. A Ford Pilot driven by the Comte de Monte Real and M.J. Palmer was second and the Jaguar Mark V of C. Vardi and A. Young, which started from Glasgow was third. Fourth was a Citroen 6, and fifth Louis Chiron in another Delahaye. Chiron was fastest in the speed test averaging 51mph and reaching 100mph in places. Tying for sixth place was a Ford Pilot driven by Ken Wharton and the leading Jowett Jupiter which, driven by Ellison and Robinson, won the 1.5 litre class. Gordon Wilkins and Raymond Baxter came second in the 1.5 class with another Jupiter. The Concours de Confort Class was won again by Mike Couper, this time with a 4.5 litre Bentley and, amongst other prize winners was a Jaguar, a Daimler, a Humber, a Hillman and a Sunbeam Talbot. *Motor Sport* noted that the rally had been highly successful and that it had done no harm at all to British prestige, adding that the Ford Pilot had shown itself to be a sound long-distance touring car, and that the Jaguar Mark V had proved to be a truly great car even though it lacked the twin overhead camshaft engine of the XK120 and the Mark VII.

Mille Miglia

Enzo Ferrari entered three open sports cars for Alberto Ascari, Dorino Serafini and Vittorio Marzotto and a fourth closed sports tourer for Luigi Villoresi. Gianno Marzotto,who had won in 1950, designed a new car for the race with a Ferrari 212 chassis. In the days before wind tunnels he streamlined it by 'optical intuition!' In response Enzo refused to send him a lower and wider radiator so that the front of the car was higher than Marzotto had intended. In 1951 the section of the course between Rome and Florence was altered so that it passed through Viterbo and Siena. In driving rain Gianno Marzotto took an early lead as his car proved to be more manageable in those conditions than Villoresi's more powerful Ferrari. Ascari crashed into the crowd a few miles before Brescia and, sadly, one spectator died later of his injuries. Then, while he continued to lead the race, Gianno Marzotto experienced a problem which he believed was caused by a broken rear axle. A hasty examination of the tyres seemed to eliminate the possibility that they were the cause and so he retired. Thus it was Luigi Villoresi who won the race with a time of 12 hours, 50 mins 18 secs. Second was the Bracco/Maglioli Lancia Aurelia, third the Scotti/Ruspaggiari Ferrari, fourth the P. Marzotto/Marini Ferrari, fifth the Ippocampo/Mori Lancia Aurelia and sixth the Bonetto/Casnaghi Alfa Romeo. Of the 325 starters 175 finished the race. After the race it was discovered Mazotto's Ferrari had in fact only required a replacement tyre to make it race worthy again.

Le Mans

William Lyons brought a team of XK120C Type Jaguars to Le Mans in 1951 with his Team Manager Lofty England. Compared to the XK120s of the previous year they were lighter, faster and built with Le Mans in mind. David Brown arrived with his team of DB2s and Team Manager John Wyer. Both Lyons and David Brown clearly meant business and the race was to produce a very good result for the British cars.

The Walker/ Whitehead C Type Jaguar winning the Le Mans 24 Hour Race in 1951, the first British car to win the race since 1930.

Froilan Gonzales led at the end of the first lap, his Talbot being a T26GS (Grand Prix) Lago Talbot. He was followed at that stage by Stirling Moss' C Type Jaguar and Tom Cole's Allard, but after 20 minutes it was the Jaguar that led. At 8 00pm the Jaguars of Moss/ Fairman and Johnson/Biondetti lay first and second with Juan Fangio now driving the Gonzales' Talbot in third position. However, in the course of the night the leading Jaguars both retired after Moss had established a new lap record at 105.1mph, and the leading Talbot suffered a serious delay at its pit after an electrical fire. In the morning the remaining works Jaguar of Peter Walker/Peter Whitehead led from a Cunningham while the Lance Macklin/ Eric Thompson DB2 Aston Martin was in third place. At midday the Cunningham lost an hour in its pit and this enabled the Aston Martin to take its place, which it held until it was overhauled by the Talbot of Meyrat/Maitesse. The Peter Whitehead/ Peter Walker Jaguar won the race at an average speed of 93.50mph, covering a distance of 2,243.9 miles in the 24 hours. In addition a works Jaguar XK120 driven by Lawre/Walker finished in eleventh place. The DB2 of Lance Macklin and Eric Thompson was third and their team mates George Abecassis/Brian Shawe-Taylor 5th. A Nash Healey driven by Tony Rolt/Duncan Hamilton finished 6th and two additional DB2s entered by Aston Martin finished 10th and 13th. Many years later Duncan Hamilton told me that he had enjoyed the protection from the elements offered by the saloon Nash Healey. Motor Sport commented that the C Type Jaguars reached 160mph at 5,800 rpm and suggested that William Lyons might well be tempted to enter Formula 1. The winning Jaguar finished nine laps ahead of the Talbot of Megrat and Mairesse. A second Talbot driven by Levegh and Mareland was 4th and the Ferraris of Chinetti/Lucas and Chiron/Taruffi were 8th and 9th. The 1,100 – 1,500cc Class was won by the Jowett Jupiter of Becquart and Wilkins and the 5,000 – 8,000cc by the Cunningham of Walters and Fitch.

1952
The unrivalled Ferrari 500

A T THE END of 1951 the writing had been on the wall for the 159 Alfa Romeos because they had reached the end of their development and were already matched by the 4.5 litre unsupercharged Ferrari 375s. So, having enjoyed a period of dominance in the years immediately after the war, it was no surprise to anyone when the decision was taken by Alfa Romeo to withdraw from racing rather than face either losing further races or embarking upon the expense of producing an entirely new car. Sadly, Raymond Mays could offer the F.I.A. no assurance that B.R.M. would be able to field a team of competitive and reliable cars throughout 1952, Mercedes Benz had decided to focus its attention on the new Formula, and so the decision was made to adopt Formula 2 for the new Season even though the new 2.5 unsupercharged/750cc supercharged Formula wouldn't come in until 1954. It was a body blow to B.R.M. enthusiasts as it meant that the V16 cars would be relegated to minor Formula Libre events on unsuitable circuits. B.R.M.'s only real hope for the future lay in producing a car for the 1954 Formula, and the prospect of a V8 750cc supercharged B.R.M. seemed to be not entirely impossible.

Alberto Ascari

Formula 2 presented the prospect of closely fought contests from the very start of the 1952 Season. No one had taken the 500cc supercharged option but there were several 2 litre cars in Italy, Britain and France which were ready for the fray. First and foremost was the 4 cylinder Tipo 500 Ferrari which had been designed by Aurelio Lampredi. Then Count Orsi offered the entirely new 6 cylinder A6GCM, which would make its first appearance at Monza, and there were the 2 litre Maserati-Plates with 4CLT frames which could be brought into contention from the beginning of the year. France could offer the Gordinis and, from Great Britain, there were the H.W.M.s, Connaughts, Cooper-Bristols and the G Type E.R.A. The reality is that, with the works Maseratis arriving too late in the year to make an impact, the Ferraris were to sweep the board. Yet the British and French cars brought interest and colour to the proceedings and Formula 2 produced full starting grids while also preparing the way for the new Formula.

THE WORLD CHAMPIONSHIP SEASON
The Swiss Grand Prix. Berne: May 18

The first World Championship Grand Prix for Formula 2 cars was at Berne and there was a large entry of Italian, British, French and German cars. It suggested that the new regime would bring about close competitive racing but it soon became clear that Ferrari would be the dominant force. Alberto Ascari was in America for the Indianapolis 500 Mile Race which was to take place on May 30 where, after being 21st in practice with a specially prepared works 4.5 litre Ferrari, he retired on lap 41 with wheel failure after running in 8th place. Luigi Villoresi was recovering from injuries sustained in a recent road accident, and so the three Ferraris were driven by Giuseppe Farina, Piero Taruffi and Andre Simon.

Piero Taruffi winning the Swiss Grand Prix in a Ferrari 500.

Farina was fastest in practice followed Taruffi while alongside them on the front row was Robert Manzon's Gordini. Simon's third works Ferrari and Rudi Fischer's privately entered Ferrari occupied the second row. Then came Peter Collins (H.W.M.) Jean Behra (Gordini) and Toulo de Graffenried (Maserati-Plate) in the third row. The H.W.M.s of Stirling Moss and George Abecassis were immediately behind them and, in row five Prince Bira (Gordini) Lance Macklin (H.W.M.) and Ken Wharton (Fraser Nash). Row six was occupied by Hans Stuck (A.F.M.) and Alan Brown (Cooper-Bristol); row seven by Toni Ulmen (Veritas-Meteor) Eric Brandon (Cooper-Bristol) and Harry Schell (Maserati-Plate). Peter Hirt (Ferrari) and Louis Rosier (Ferrari) came next and Max de Terra (Simca-Gordini) took up the rear.

Farina led for the first 17 laps, followed by Taruffi, and when Farina's car retired with a failed magneto on lap 17 his team mate's car led until the end of the race. The third works Ferrari was called in so that Simon could hand over to Farina but it also retired with magneto trouble on lap 51. Behra was in second place behind the flying Taruffi but he was overtaken by Fischer when the Gordini's exhaust pipe had to be replaced. Behind the leading three, Wharton finished fourth, Brown fifth, de Graffenried sixth, Hirt seventh, and Brandon eighth. All the H.W.M.s had to be withdrawn after Abecassis and Collins experienced broken De Dion tubes. Taruffi led Fischer across the finishing line by three minutes at an average speed of 92.799mph. He also established the fastest lap of the race at 96.303mph. Critics complained that the Formula 2 cars were slow and unexciting compared with the bigger Formula 1 cars of the previous year.

Monaco Grand Prix. Monte Carlo: June 2

The authorities decided that the Monaco Grand Prix would be a 100 lap race for sports cars in 1952 and so it didn't count towards the World Championship. Pierre Levegh was fastest in practice with his Type 150C Talbot and Stirling Moss second fastest in his works C Type Jaguar. On lap 17 Reg Parnell's Aston Martin DB3 dropped oil on the track, causing a multiple pile up which eliminated a number of cars, including Moss's Jaguar and Hume's Chrysler Allard. Moss, who had led at the start, was disqualified after receiving outside assistance to move his car from where it had been obstructing the track and the race was won by Vittotio Marzotto's Ferrari followed by four more 2.7 litre Ferraris. Sadly Luigi Fagioli died from injuries sustained when he had crashed in practice for the race.

The Belgian Grand Prix. Spa: June 22

Alberto Ascari returned in good time for the race at Spa and took pole position with his team mates Giuseppe Farina and Piero Taruffi completing the front row. Robert Manzon's Gordini was a full six seconds slower than the third Ferrari and was on the second row with Jean Behra's similar car. Next came Mike Hawthorn (Cooper-Bristol), Ken Wharton (Fraser Nash) and Paul Frere (H.W.M.). The fourteen remaining cars included Stirling Moss in his brand new Bristol engined G Type E.R.A. A new engine had to be flown to Belgium in a Silver City Bristol Freight when the E.R.A.'s original engine seized up during practice. He would retire on the second lap of the race when this engine also seized up. In extremely wet conditions Ascari led from Farina at the start but both were passed by Behra who held on to his lead until spinning on the second lap. Peter Collins' H.W.M. was eliminated on lap 3 with a sheered drive shaft and Wharton spun his Frazer Nash on the eleventh lap at Stavelot, sustaining severe cuts on his back from barbed wire in the process. Taruffi, after making a faltering start, eventually caught and overtook Behra to take third place on lap 14 but then lost it when he spun and collected the Gordini in the process. As a result of this the Ferraris of Ascari and Farina were followed across the line after an interval

Mike Hawthorn bringing his Cooper-Bristol home in fourth place at Spa.

by Manzon's Gordini. Hawthorn (Cooper-Bristol) in his first Continental race, was fourth, Frere (H.W.M) fifth and Brown (Cooper-Bristol) sixth. The H.W.M.s of Macklin, Laurent, and Gaze finished 11th, 12th and 15th. Ascari's winning speed was 103.125mph. He also recorded the fastest lap of the race at 107.069mph.

The French Grand Prix. Rouen: July 6

John Cooper won the Formula 3 race which preceded the Grand Prix at Rouen in his Cooper Norton. Then, as the cars lined up for the three hour main event, the three Ferraris of Alberto Ascari, Giuseppe Farina and Piero Taruffi, each with new and longer radiator cowls, were at the front of the starting grid, as had been the case at Spa. Immediately behind them once again were the Gordinis of Jean Behra and Robert Manzon. The rest of the field was composed of three more Gordinis, three H.W.M.s, two Maserati-Plates, an Alta, a Cooper-Bristol, a Maserati and four privately entered Ferraris. Ascari and Farina led Behra away from the start and the Gordini spun out of contention on the third lap enabling Taruffi to assume third place. The three Ferraris completed the race unchallenged in that order without stopping either for fuel or tyres. Manzon, who had been lapped before half distance, was fourth, Maurice Trintignant (Gordini) fifth, Peter Collins' H.W.M. sixth, Behra seventh, Philippe Etancelin (Maserati) eighth, Lance Macklin (H.W.M.) ninth, Yves Giraud-Cabantous (H.W.M.) tenth, Rudi Fischer/Peter Hirt (Ferrari) eleventh and Franco Comotti (Ferrari) twelfth. Ascari won at 80.131mph and established the fastest lap of the race at 83.071mph.

The British Grand Prix. Silverstone: July 19

As might have been expected the British teams were fully represented at Silverstone for the British Grand Prix with the Cooper-Bristols and H.W.M.s being joined by the A Type Connaughts with revised exhaust systems and new found speed, the G Type E.R.A. and an Aston–Butterworth.

Farina, Ascari and Taruffi yet again secured the first three places on the grid with Manzon's Gordini alongside them.

The starting grid

R. Manzon	P. Taruffi	A. Ascari	G. Farina
Gordini	Ferrari	Ferrari	Ferrari
1 min 55 secs	1 min 53 secs	1 min 50 secs	1 min 50 secs

J.M. Hawthorn	R. Parnell	K. Downing
Cooper-Bristol	Cooper-Bristol	Connaught
1 min 56 secs	1 min 56 secs	1 min 56 secs

D. Hamilton	B. Bira	E. Thompson	D. Poore
H.W.M	Gordini	Connaught	Connaught
1 min 57 secs	1 min 57 secs	1 min 57 secs	1 min 56 secs

P. Collins	A. Brown	A.G. Whitehead
H.W.M	Cooper-Bristol	Alta
1 min 58 secs	1 min 58 secs	1 min 58 secs

E. Brandon	K. McAlpine	S. Moss	R. Fischer
Cooper-Bristol	Connaught	E.R.A	Ferrari
2 min 00 secs	2 min 00 secs	1 min 59 secs	1 min 58 secs

M. Trintignant	P. Whitehead	R. Salvadori
Gordini	Ferrari	Ferrari
2 min 00 secs	2 min 00 secs	2 min 00 secs

T.A.D. Crook	P. Hirt	J. Claes	D. Murray
Fraser-Nash	Ferrari	Gordini	Cooper-Bristol
2 min 03 secs	2 min 03 secs	2 min 02 secs	2 min 02 secs

G. Bianco	H. Cantoni	F.A.O. Gaze
Maserati	Maserati	H.W.M
2 min 07 secs	2 min 06 secs	2 min 05 secs

H. Schell	E. de Graffenried	W. Aston	L. Macklin
Maserati-Plate	Maserati-Plate	Aston-Butterworth	H.W.M
		3 min 28 secs	2 min 08 secs

The two Maserati-Plates failed to practice.

Ken Downing was fourth fastest alongside the Cooper-Bristols of Parnell and Hawthorn and the Connaughts of Dennis Poore and Eric Thompson were next up. Duncan Hamilton was fastest of the four H.W.M.s in 11th place and Moss was only 16th in the uncompetitive E.R.A. At the end of the first lap the crowd was delighted to see the Connaughts of Poore and Downing in third and fourth places behind Ascari and Farina. The two Connaughts held on to Farina but Taruffi, having overtaken Thompson, passed Poore when he stopped for fuel on lap 15. Farina dropped back after calling at his pit with a misfire on lap 27 to

Stirling Moss driving the G Type E.R.A. in the British Grand Prix.

Alberto Ascari winning the British Grand Prix on July 19th with his Ferrari 500 while lapping Harry Schell's Maserati Plate.

have his plugs changed. Ascari won the race comfortably from Taruffi who was followed by Hawthorn. After these three came Poore, Thompson and Farina. There were twenty-two finishers, the last one, Alan Brown, being 16 laps behind the winner. The winner's speed was 90.92mph and Ascari recorded the fastest lap of the race at 94.08mph.

Results

1. A Ascari Ferrari 90.92mph
2. P. Taruffi Ferrari 1 lap behind
3. J.M. Hawthorn Cooper-Bristol 2 laps behind
4. D. Poore Connaught
5. E. Thompson Connaught 3 laps behind
6. G. Farina Ferrari
7. R. Parnell Cooper-Bristol
8. R. Salvadori Ferrari
9. K. Downing Connaught
10. P. Whitehead Ferrari 4 laps behind
11. B. Bira Gordini
12. A. G. Whitehead Alta 5 laps behind
13. R. Fischer Ferrari
14. J. Claes Gordini 6 laps behind
15. L. Macklin H.W.M.
16. K. McAlpine Connaught
17. H. Schell Maserati-Plate 7 laps behind
18. G. Bianco Maserati 8 laps behind
19. E. De Graffenried Maserati-Plate 9 laps behind
20. E. Brandon Cooper-Bristol
21. T.A.D. Crook Frazer-Nash 10 laps behind
22. A. Brown Cooper-Bristol 19 laps behind

Retirements: H. Cantoni Maserati with brake trouble on lap 1, P.Hirt Ferrari with brake failure on lap 3, R. Manzon Gordini with clutch trouble on lap 9, D. Murray Cooper-Bristol with engine trouble on lap 14. F.A.O. Gaze H.W.M. with blown gasket on lap 20, M. Trintignant Gordini with gearbox trouble on lap 22, S. Moss E.R.A. with engine failure on lap 36, D. Hamilton H.W.M. with engine trouble on lap 44, and P. Collins H.W.M. with ignition trouble on lap 73.

The German Grand Prix. Nurburgring: August 3

Predictably there was a large German entry at the Nurburgring and it consisted of an A.F.M., seven Veritases, two B.M.W.s, a B.M.W.-Reif, a B.M.W.-Heck and an A.F.M. The British contingent was confined to the H.W.M. team which, arrived after racing at Caen the previous weekend, ill prepared. The Ferraris of Alberto Ascari and Piero Taruffi had new engines with forward mounted magnetos while Giuseppe Farina's car had an earlier engine. Ascari was fastest in practice followed by Farina but they were joined on the front row of the grid by the Gordinis of Maurice Trintignant and Robert Manzon. Taruffi was fifth fastest and on the second row. Ascari led Farina at the start and Taruffi passed Manzon to run in third place on the second lap. Then Manzon lost a wheel on lap 9 and Ascari stopped for oil on the 17th lap. This enabled Farina to snatch the lead but he was overhauled by Ascari who won at an average speed of 82.2mph. Farina finished 14 seconds behind Ascari and Fischer and Taruffi were third and fourth in their Ferraris. The next cars to finish were Jean Behra's Gordini, Laurent's Ferrari and Riess' Veritas. The H.W.M.s of Tony Gaze, Paul Frere, and Johnny Claes all failed to finish. Ascari posted the fastest lap of the race at 84.33mph.

The Dutch Grand Prix. Zandvoort: August 17

The new circuit at Zandvoort staged its first World Championship Grand Prix on August 17. Luigi Villoresi returned to the Ferrari team in place of Piero Taruffi and was fourth in practice and while Alberto Ascari and Giuseppe Farina were almost inevitably first and second, Mike Hawthorn was a highly creditable third fastest in his Cooper-Bristol. Three Gordinis were 5th, 6th and 8th on the starting grid and it was Ken Wharton's Frazer Nash that came between them. The H.W.M.s of Lance Macklin and Duncan Hamilton were next, on the fourth row of the grid and in amongst the rest of the field was a third H.W.M. driven

Alberto Ascari winning the Dutch Grand Prix with his 2 litre unsupercharged Ferrari.

by Dries van de Lof, Downing's Connaught and Moss' G Type E.R.A. At the start of the race Hawthorn succeeded in getting between Ascari's Ferrari and the Ferraris of Farina and Villoresi, but by the third lap the three Ferraris were at the front with Ascari drawing away from the field. Hawthorn remained the best of the rest finishing fourth with the Gordinis of Manzon and Trintignant and the H.W.M.s of Hamilton and Macklin next up. Ascari won at 81.13mph and his fastest lap was set at 85.41mph.

The Ferraris of Alberto Ascari
and Giuseppe Farina at
Monza.

The Italian Grand Prix. Monza: September 7

The entry for the Italian Grand Prix at Monza was oversubscribed and most notable
amongst the entrants were the new 6 cylinder twin plug works A6GCM Maseratis of Froilan
Gonzales, Felice Bonetto and Franco Rol which took on the five works Ferraris of Alberto
Ascari, Luigi Villoresi, Giuseppe Farina, Piero Taruffi and Andre Simon. There was also a

Froilan Gonzales in his
A6GCM Maserati at Monza.

Cisitalia, an OSCA, three Connaughts driven by Stirling Moss, Dennis Poore and Kenneth McAlpine, and four Cooper-Bristols in the hands of Mike Hawthorn, Eric Brandon, Alan Brown, and Ken Wharton whose car was entered by Ecurie Ecosse. Sadly the three H.W.M.s were amongst the nine cars which failed to qualify for the race as the entry was limited to the 24 cars. Sensationally it was Gonzales who led when the flag fell with his Maserati having come through from the second row on the grid. He was followed by Ascari's Ferrari and Trintignant's Gordini, and Gonzales proceeded to draw away while Villoresi moved up to third place and then overtook Ascari. Behind the first three cars there was a good deal of close racing involving occasional high speed contact, but everyone managed to stay on the road. When Gonzales came in to re-fuel the three Ferraris of Ascari, Villoresi and Farina led the race but Gonzales was soon chasing hard after them and recovered to finish in third

Stirling Moss in an A Type Connaught during the Italian Grand Prix.

place. Bonetto finished fifth, Wharton (Cooper-Bristol) was ninth, Poore (Connaught) and the Cooper-Bristols of Brandon and Brown were twelfth, thirteenth and fifteenth. The performance of the new A6GCM Maseratis was a shot in the arm for the interim Formula and suggested that Ferrari would not have it all its own way in 1953. Ascari's winning speed was 110.038mph and he and Gonzales both produced fastest laps at 111.758mph.

The 1952 World Championship

It had become apparent early in the year that Ferraris would be dominant and that Alberto Ascari would be the new World Champion. The first four places were taken by Ferrari drivers, Alberto Ascari having gained 36 points, Giuseppe Farina 24, Piero Taruffi 22, and Rudi Fischer 10. Mike Hawthorn was fourth equal with 10 points and Robert Manzon was sixth with 9. Such was the dominance of the Ferraris that Troy Ruttman in the Agajanian Special came seventh with his win at Indianapolis.

NON CHAMPIONSHIP EVENTS
The Ulster Trophy Race. Dundrod: June 7

Immediately after the Italian Grand Prix in 1951, when the two B.R.M.s had to be scratched from the race because of gearbox failures, Stirling Moss and Juan Fangio tested the cars on the famous Italian circuit with a view to eliminating all the problems that continued to afflict

Luigi Villoresi driving the works 4.5 litre "Indianapolis" Ferrari during the Formula Libre Race at Silverstone.

them. It had been the last opportunity for the B.R.M.s to compete with the Alfa Romeos and Ferraris in a major Grand Prix. In 1952 the V16 1½ litre supercharged cars were relegated to Formula Libre events as Alfa Romeo had withdrawn from racing altogether and the race organisers were not convinced that the B.R.M.s could offer a sustained challenge to Ferrari.

George Abecassis in his H.W.M. in close company with Baron de Graffenried during the *Daily Express* International Trophy race at Silverstone.

Mike Hawthorn winning the Sussex International Trophy Race at Goodwood on Whit Monday in his Cooper-Bristol.

An Aston Martin DB3 with John Wyer in the foreground before the Goodwood Nine Hours Race in 1952.

So Juan Fangio and Stirling Moss found themselves in Dundrod on June 7 competing for the Ulster Trophy over 34 laps of the 7.5 mile circuit in the B.R.M.s, six days after the cars' further failure at Albi. The cars were unready when they arrived at Dundrod and it would have been better if they had stayed away. Fangio's car stalled at the start while Moss' clutch burnt out on the starting line. Both were pushed off but on the first lap Stirling encountered Fangio running downhill towards him in reverse. On the second lap the gear knob came away in Stirling's hand and his car began to overheat. His race ended after four laps. Fangio ran in third place behind Piero Taruffi's Thin Wall Special Ferrari and Mike Hawthorn's 2 litre Cooper Bristol until he stopped on lap 25 with fuel starvation. It meant that Stirling Moss would never drive the V16 again.

The Monte Carlo Rally

The 1952 Monte Carlo Rally was won by Sydney Allard in one of his own 4.4 litre P1 Allard saloons, his co driver being Guy Warburton. Having secured a drive from the Routes Group, Stirling Moss was second overall in a Sunbeam Talbot 90 saloon which he shared with Desmond Scannall and John Cooper of Autocar. Moss went on later in the year to win a Coupe des Alpes in the Alpine Rally, a triumph he was to repeat in the following two years.

E. and R. Sneath competing in the crucial Regularity Test during the 1952 Monte Carlo Rally with their Sunbeam Talbot.

The Concours de Confort was won by the Mark VI Bentley of Mike Cooper. Walter Waring's Mark VII Jaguar won the over 1500cc Class.

The Monte Carlo Rally was an event which featured strongly in the motor racing calendar in the 1950s and success in the rally had an immediate effect upon sales, particularly where a small manufacturer like Allard was concerned. Its appeal lay in the extreme conditions which were often encountered on the way and the possibility that either

B G Appe

Walter Waring's Mark VII
Jaguar during the 1952 Monte
Carlo Rally.

Sydney Allard, Guy Warburton
and Tom Lush winning the
1952 Monte Carlo Rally in their
P1 Allard.

this or mechanical failure would prevent many competitors getting to Monte Carlo at all.
Of the 328 starters in 1952 only 163 reached their destination. A Jowett Javelin was
equipped with snow chains, an extra fuel tank, fog lights, a roof-mounted spot light, and
projecting head lamp covers to shield the driver from the glare of the snow. *Motor Sport*
reported that in 1952 the rally was 'a story of crashes and ditching in the snow and ice from
Clemont Ferrand onwards. Hereafter conditions were terrible and car after car either
collided with objects mobile or stationary or slid into snow banks and ditches'. The Glasgow
contingent had 564 miles to travel before crossing the Channel where the rally really began
in earnest. Of the British cars there were 18 Jaguars, 16 Fords, 15 Sunbeam Talbots, 13
Jowett Javelins, 11 Austins, 9 Rileys, 7 Hillmans, 6 Vauxhalls, 6 Allards, 5 Humbers, 4

Morris, 3 Bentleys, 2 Bristols, 2 Alvis, 2 Singers, and single entries of an MG, Wolseley, Lanchester, Lagonda, AC and Daimler.

Stirling Moss started from Monte Carlo and his course took him on a circuitous route around Europe before finishing where it started. In *All My Races* he describes how, in the course of the Regularity section over the mountains, he slid his Sunbeam Talbot into a snow bank and, not knowing how long he had taken to extricate it, couldn't know how much time he had to make up in order to arrive on time. He was 28 seconds too early whereas Sydney Allard was just 24 seconds out!

Sydney Allard wrote afterwards that the roads were covered with snow and ice between Glasgow and Carlisle as was also the case in Wales. Having been escorted through Paris by police motorcyclists, he encountered snow again and found that the mountain roads had narrowed with steep banks of snow on each side. He had memorised certain land marks the day before the Regularity Test but found that a heavy fall of snow had hidden them from sight! Moss noted that his Sunbeam Talbot passed more expensive European models with ease and averaged between 22 and 26 mpg. *The Motor* reported that Sidney Allard came across his wife's Allard parked by the road side with all its lights blazing near the Auvergne mountains. Pulling up alongside he shouted, 'Are you alright?' His wife and two sisters-in-law chorused 'No!' 'Oh,' replied Allard benevolently, 'pity,' and drove on!

The Mille Miglia

Added interest was brought to the Mille Miglia in 1952 by the appearance of the new 300SL Mercedes Benz with gull doors. With a degree of thoroughness which was reminiscent of the Silver Arrows of the 1930s, they arrived many weeks before the race and were driven over the course a dozen times. Ferrari's response was the Tipo 225 Sports Ferraris of Eugenio Castellotti, Paola Marzotto, Vittorio Marzotto and Scotti. However Giovanni Bracco had a prototype 2.7 litre V12 Ferrari with a Coupe body by Vignale. It was Bracco

Wisdom and Hume approaching the Rome control in their Aston Martin DB2 during the 1952 Mille Miglia.

who led initially but for most of the race it was Karl Kling's 300SL at the front. Hermann Lang retired when his Mercedes went off the road and the great Rudolf Caracciola had difficulty in trying to shake off the DB2 Aston Martin driven by George Abecassis. Then, during a tremendous battle with the Mercedes team, Bracco regained the lead before Bologna only to be repassed by Kling. Bracco's tyres were down to the canvas and, as an amateur, he had to finish the race on tyres of an unsuitable size for the car. In spite of this he to managed to get in front once more, averaging 93mph on the Futa Pass. So the race went to the V12 Ferrari of Bracco and Rolfe who took 12 hours 9 minutes and 45 seconds to complete the 1000 miles at an average speed of 79.9mph. It was a famous win by an amateur. The Kling/Klenk Mercedes was second, a 2 litre Lancia Aurelia driven by Fagioli and Borghi third, and Caracciola's Mercedes Benz fourth. The over 2000cc Grand Touring category was won by Tommy Wisdom's DB2 Aston Martin which covered the course in 14 hours, 29 minutes and 40 seconds. Reg Parnell's DB2 ran out of fuel after hitting a stone bridge and Donald Healey crashed after a tyre burst on his Healey.

Le Mans

Mercedes Benz returned to Le Mans in 1952 with a team of 300SL cars and team manager Alfred Neubauer to direct them. Their meticulous preparation bred despondency amongst all its rivals. The German team had five cars to choose from, one of which had an experimental air brake which would be introduced in 1955. The 300SLs were not the only new cars promised for the race although, sadly, the Alfa Romeos and Pegasos failed to arrive. Jaguar did come, with a team of C Types with elongated noses and sweeping tails which looked impressive and caused excitement although they turned out to be a disaster. Stirling

Pierre Levegh's Talbot being hounded by the two 300SL Mercedes at Le Mans.

Moss, having encountered the Mercedes in the Mille Miglia earlier in the year, warned Lofty England that the Jaguars would need to find more speed to beat them. Many years later Duncan Hamilton told me that he had disagreed at the time. The problem was that the modified cooling system was ineffective and desperate attempts to improve it during practice failed to remedy the situation. The Jaguars would all be out of the race in the early hours. The Peter Whitehead/Ian Stewart car retired in the second hour, the Stirling Moss/Peter Walker car in the third and the Tony Rolt/Duncan Hamilton car in the fourth. A Cunningham led at the start of the race, but it was soon overtaken by Ascari's Ferrari who nevertheless soon retired with clutch trouble. Then it was Simon's turn to lead in a 4.1 litre Ferrari until 8 p.m. when Jean Behra's 2.2 litre Gordini took his place at the head of the field. At that stage the leading Mercedes was that of Karl Kling/Klenk in second place while the Hermann Lang/Riess car was 7th behind Pierre Levegh's Talbot. Kling's Mercedes retired with electrical problems and Levegh lay second to the Gordini and, by midnight the remaining two Mercedes were running in 3rd and 4th positions, content to play a waiting game. At 3 30 a.m the Gordini stopped with brake failure and so the order was Talbot,

Stirling Moss driving the streamlined but overheating C Type Jaguar at le Mans in 1952.

The Hay/Clark Bentley which came twenty-second at Le Mans.

Mercedes, Mercedes. The remaining DB3 Aston Martin of Macklin/Collins was 4th and Sydney Allard, in one of his own cars fifth, until, at 6 30 a.m. the Allard stopped with no brakes and a damaged shock absorber. Levegh, driving the entire race single handed, was four laps ahead of the German cars. Unknown to everyone else at the time, he was nursing his car's stricken crankshaft and it broke with only 55 minutes to go. So it was a triumph for the 300SL Mercedes Benz of Lang/Riess and Helfrich/Niedermayer although luck as well as Teutonic planning had played a part. The Nash Healey of Brian Johnson/Tommy Wisdom was 3rd, and the Cunningham of Cunningham/Spears 4th. The three DB3 Aston Martins driven by Lance Macklin/Peter Collins, Dennis Poore/Griffith and Reg Parnell/ Eric Thompson all retired during the course of the race but an Aston Martin DB2 driven by Clark/Keen finished 3rd to the Mercedes in the 3 litre class and 7th overall. A second DB2 driven by Mann/Morris Goodall retired. A sole M.G.A. retired and a Bentley finished in 22nd place.

The Type R1 Jowett Jupiters of Gatsonides/van Zuylen and Hadley/Wise at Le Mans. Neither finished but the Becquart/Wilkins Jupiter won its class.

1953
The A6SSG Maserati joins the party

This was the last year before the new Formula 1 would come into force. Juan Fangio, recovered from his accident at Monza the previous year which had left him in plaster for five months, was fit to drive for Maserati with his fellow Argentinian Froilan Gonzales and they were given an improved version of the A6GCM, designed by Giaocchino Colombo and called the A6SSG. A great deal of interest was focused on whether the Maserati would prove to be a match for the Tipo 500 Ferraris which had also been given increased power. In Britain Cooper had produced a new car with an Alta engine for Stirling Moss but the new B Type Connaught was not ready for the start of the new Season.

THE WORLD CHAMPIONSHIP SEASON
The Argentine Grand Prix. Buenos Aires:
January 18

The first race of the year was held in Buenos Aires and Ferrari and Maserati each produced four cars for the event. Sixteen cars lined up for the race in all and Alberto Ascari (Ferrari), Juan Fangio (Maserati), Luigi Villoresi (Ferrari) and Giuseppe Farina (Ferrari) occupied the front row of the grid in that order. Fangio drove a 1952 Maserati while the Ferrari drivers had Enzo's latest cars. Froilan Gonzales (Maserati) was fifth and Mike Hawthorn, driving a works Ferrari

Stirling Moss.

for the first time was sixth, his car being finished in British Racing Green. Felice Bonetto was at the back of the grid with the fourth Maserati, rueing the fact that the new cars were not yet available. Hawthorn made a poor start and was dismayed to see his team mates drawing away from him. The race was led by Ascari followed by Villoresi, Gonzales, Fangio, Bonetto, Farina and Villoresi with Bonetto driving with great determination and verve. Behind Ascari, Hawthorn and Villoresi proceeded to gain both ground and places but on lap 32 Farina had to swerve to avoid a spectator who was running across the track and consequently ploughed into the crowd. Fifteen spectators were killed and others badly injured. Two more spectators were inadvertently killed by the ambulance as it rushed to the scene. The race continued and Fangio retired with a broken universal joint on lap 36. Robert Manzon held on to second place with his Gordini until he lost a wheel. Then

Gonzales took over second place until he had to stop for fuel. The result of this tragic race was that Ascari won at a speed of 78.145mph and he was followed by Villoresi, Gonzales and Hawthorn. Cooper-Bristols came 8th and 9th in the hands of John Barber and Alan Brown. The fastest lap was recorded by Ascari at 80.735mph.

The Dutch Grand Prix. Zandvoort: June 7

Built on sand dunes, Zandvoort was covered by a thin layer of sand blown in from the dunes by the wind, and the situation was further aggravated by loose grit following a recent resurfacing of the course. This became a problem as the grit was thrown up by the rear wheels of cars into the faces of the following drivers, and wide shields were specially constructed which spanned the space between the mirrors to protect the Maserati drivers. The new A6SSG Maseratis with revised bodies were present for Juan Fangio, Froilan Gonzales, and Felice Bonetto while Toulo de Graffenried drove the earlier version. However Alberto Ascari was faster than any of them in practice with his Ferrari, followed by Fangio, Luigi Villoresi, Gonzales, Mike Hawthorn and de Graffenried. It promised a close race between the two teams but at the start the three Ferraris of Ascari, Giuseppe Farina and Villoresi headed the field, the last two having squeezed Fangio's Maserati out so that he was almost forced to stop. Hawthorn was immediately behind Fangio, and Stirling Moss, now driving an A Type Connaught, was up in 7th place at the end of the first lap. Gonzales moved up after a slow start and, after having to retire with a broken rear axle, took over Bonetto's car. He became the hero of the day as he slid his borrowed Maserati round the bends, shaking his fist at the other drivers ahead of him until he only had the Ferraris of Ascari and Farina in front to tackle. Ascari won at 81.04mph from Farina and the Bonetto/ Gonzales Maserati. Hawthorn was fourth and de Graffenried fifth. Peter Collins (H.W.M.) and Moss were eighth and ninth. The other British entrants, Lance Macklin (H.W.M), Ken Wharton (Cooper-Bristol), and Kenneth McAlpine (Connaught) were all forced to retire. Ascari's winning speed was 81.04mph and Farina finished 10.8 seconds behind him. Villoresi recorded the fastest lap of the race at 83.15mph.

The Belgian Grand Prix. Spa: June 21

At Spa Juan Fangio and Froilan Gonzales were first and third on the starting grid with Alberto Ascari's Ferrari sandwiched between them. The order behind them was Giuseppe Farina, Luigi Villoresi in Ferraris, Onofre Marimon, in a brand new privately entered Maserati finished in the blue and yellow of Argentina, Mike Hawthorn in the fourth Ferrari, Maurice Trintignant (Gordini) and Toulo de Graffenried in another privately entered Maserati. Johnny Claes was 10th fastest in a third works Maserati. Further back on the grid were the three H.W.M.s of Paul Frere, Peter Collins and Lance Macklin. At the fall of the flag the Maseratis of Gonzales and Fangio led Ascari, who seemed to have been put off his stroke by having his rivals on either side of him, and he was followed by the Ferraris of Farina, Villoresi and Hawthorn. Gonzales was still leading Fangio at the end of the first lap and pulled away from him, the race apparently firmly in his pocket. Marimon overtook Hawthorn and Villoresi and things were looking good for Maserati until Gonzales stopped on lap 12 with a broken accelerator pedal and, soon afterwards, Fangio had to surrender an unassailable lead when his engine failed on lap 13. This left Ascari in front with Hawthorn and Marimon second and third. Fangio took over Johnny Claes' Maserati on lap 14 and, taking up the chase, he drove to such good effect that he was third to Ascari and Villoresi when they entered the last lap. Then he suddenly shot off the road when his steering failed on the last bend and eventually completed the course by ambulance, fortunately without serious injury. The Maseratis had shown tremendous promise but their day had yet to come. Another win was posted by Ascari, at an average speed of 112.456mph, and he was followed across the line by Villoresi, Marimon, de Graffenried, Trintignant (Gordini), and Hawthorn. Frere finished in tenth place with his H.W.M. while Collins and Macklin had retired with mechanical problems. Gonzales had the consolation of recording the fastest lap at 115.255mph.

The French Grand Prix. Rheims: July 5

No one could have anticipated the intense drama which was to unfold in the French Grand Prix at Rheims. The starting grid had the entirely predictable mix of Ferraris and Maseratis at the front with Alberto Ascari's Ferrari, Felice Bonetto's Maserati and Luigi Villoresi's Ferrari on the leading row. The Maseratis of Juan Fangio and Froilan Gonzales were immediately behind them and the Ferraris of Giuseppe Farina and Mike Hawthorn were with Onofre Marimon's Maserati in row three. After this came Baron Toulo de Graffenried's Maserati, Louis Rosier's Ferrari, Stirling Moss' Cooper-Alta, Elle Bayol's OSCA, Bob Gerard's and Ken Wharton's Cooper-Bristols and numerous H.W.M.s, Connaughts and Gordinis. All the Maseratis had their nose grills removed before the race and, with a light fuel load, it was Gonzales who led at the start followed by Ascari, Villoresi, Bonetto, Hawthorn and Fangio. Fangio steadily improved his position in the succeeding laps so that he was able to take the lead when Gonzales stopped for fuel. Then on lap 30 Hawthorn, having gained ground, set about catching the master. During the course of an enthralling duel which lasted for the rest of the race and kept the crowd on its toes, the two drivers swopped positions lap and lap, their cars often side by side and only inches apart down the long straights. In the meantime Gonzales was gaining on them after his pit stop and, overtaking Marimon, proceeded to fight an equally close contest with Ascari and Farina. In the end Hawthorn won the race at a speed of 113.641mph with Fangio a mere second

Mike Hawthorn and Juan Fangio racing side by side during the French Grand Prix.

behind. Gonzales was only 0.4 of a second behind Fangio. Ascari was fourth followed by Farina, Villoresi, de Graffenried, Rosier and Marimon. The supporting cast finished in the order of Behra (Gordini), Gerard (Cooper-Bristol), Claes (Connaught), and Collins and Giraud-Cabantous (H.W.M.s). It was an historic win for Hawthorn, and justifiably described by many as the "race of the century." It also enabled Enzo Ferrari to claim that his cars were the equal of the new Maseratis on speed. Fangio scored the fastest lap of the race at 115.905mph

The British Grand Prix. Silverstone: July 18

It was too much to expect that Hawthorn would be able to pull off an equally exciting win at Silverstone two weeks later but the British crowd could be forgiven believing that he might. A close contest between the works Ferraris and Maseratis was assured as was the presence of a large contingent of British entrants. The front row defined the race with the Ferraris of Alberto Ascari and Mike Hawthorn first and third and the Maseratis of Froilan Gonzales and Juan Fangio second and fourth. Behind these were the Ferraris of Giuseppe Farina and Luigi Villoresi and Onofre Marimon's Maserati. Then came the Gordinis, Connaughts, Cooper-Bristols, Cooper-Altas and H.W.M.s.

Starting Grid

J.M. Fangio	J.M. Hawthorn	J.F. Gonzales	A. Ascari
Maserati	Ferrari	Maserati	Ferrari
1 min 50 secs	1 min 49 secs	1 min 49 secs	1 min 48 secs

O. Marimon	L. Villoresi	G. Farina
Maserati	Ferrari	Ferrari
1 min 51 secs	1 min 51 secs	1 min 50 secs

K. Wharton	A. Rolt	H. Schell	M. Trintignant
Cooper-Bristol	Connaught	Gordini	Gordini
1 min 54 secs	1 min 54 secs	1 min 52 secs	1 min 52 secs

P. Whitehead	K. McAlpine	L. Macklin
Cooper-Alta	Connaught	H.W.M
1 min 57 secs	1 min 57 secs	1 min 57 secs

F.R. Gerard	D. Hamilton	F. Bonetto	Jim Stewart
Cooper-Bristol	H.W.M	Maserati	Cooper-Bristol
2 min 02 secs	2 min 02 secs	1 min 58 secs	1 min 58 secs

A. Brown	I. Stewart	B. Bira
Cooper-Bristol	Connaught	Connaught
2 min 04 secs	2 min 04 secs	2 min 04 secs

T.A.D. Crook	L. Rosier	P. Collins	J. Behra
Cooper-Alta	Ferrari	H.W.M	Gordini
2 min 07 secs	2 min 07 secs	2 min 06 secs	2 min 04 secs

R. Salvadori	J. Fairman	E. de Graffenried
Connaught	H.W.M	Maserati
(Failed to practice)	2 min 32 secs	2 min 09 secs

Alberto Ascari winning the British Grand Prix at Silverstone in his Ferrari 500.

Ascari made an excellent start and was followed by Fangio, who would fall back after going wide at Copse Corner, Villoresi, Gonzales, Marimon and Lance Macklin's H.W.M. Macklin was soon overwhelmed by Hawthorn and Farina and the order at the front became Ascari, Gonzales, Fangio, Villoresi, Hawthorn and Marimon. Then Hawthorn spun harmlessly at Woodcote and managed to continue his forward momentum before stopping at his pit to have his car briefly checked over. Gonzales' charge at the front was interrupted when he was black flagged to have an oil leak checked but he returned to the race, after a heated exchange of words in the pits, with minimum delay. By this time the leading cars had become strung out with Ascari still leading from Fangio, Villoresi and Marimon. The last two both retired on lap 66 with mechanical problems and Farina passed Gonzales to run third. It remained Ascari's race and he was followed across the line by Fangio, Farina, Gonzales, Hawthorn and Bonetto. Ascari's average speed was 92.97mph and the fastest lap of the race was held jointed by Ascari and Gonzales at 95.79mph.

Result
1. A. Ascari Ferrari 2 hr. 50 secs
2. J.M Fangio Maserati 2 hr. 51 secs
3. G. Farina Ferrari 2 laps behind
4. J. F. Gonzales Maserati
5. J. M Hawthorn Ferrari 3 laps behind
6. F. Bonetto Maserati 8 laps behind
7. B. Bira Connaught
8. K. Wharton Cooper-Bristol 10 laps behind
9. P. Whitehead Cooper-Alta 11 claps behind
10. L. Rosier Ferrari 12 laps behind

Retirements: K. McAlpine Connaught with split radiator hose on lap 1, T. Crook Cooper-Alta with fuel starvation on lap 1, H. Schell Gordini with failed magneto on lap 6, F. R. Gerard Cooper-Bristol with fractured oil pipe on lap 12, M. Trintignant Gordini with rear axle failure on lap 15, D. Hamilton H.W.M. with clutch trouble on lap 15, I. Stewart

Connaught with ignition failure on lap 25, J. Behra Gordini with fuel pump faiture on lap 30, L. Macklin H.W.M. with clutch trouble on lap 31, E. De Graffenried Maserati with broken clutch pedal on lap 34, R. Salvadori Connaught with broken suspension on lap 51, J. Fairman H.W.M. with clutch failure on lap 54, A. Brown Cooper-Bristol with broken fan belt on lap 56, P.Collins H.W.M. after spinning on lap 57, O. Marimon Maserati with engine trouble on lap 66, L. Villoresi Ferrari with rear axle failure on lap 66, A. Rolt Connaught with broken half shaft on lap 71 and J. Stewart Cooper-Bristol after spinning on lap 80.

The German Grand Prix. Nurburgring: August 2

Would the famous Nurburgring circuit be the scene of Maserati's first win in 1953? Honours were weighted in Ferrari's favour on the starting grid, the order being Alberto Ascari (Ferrari), Juan Fangio (Maserati), Giuseppe Farina (Ferrari) and Mike Hawthorn (Ferrari). Maurice Trintignant's Gordini was alongside Luigi Villoresi's Ferrari and Felice Bonetto's Maserati in the second row. Froilan Gonzales was missing as he had injured his neck while driving a Lancia in a sports car race in Portugal the previous week. The H.W.M. entries had not been accepted because of the large number of German cars with Hans Herrmann, Willi Heeks, Wolfgang Seidel, Theo Helfrich, Oswald Karch and Erwin Bauer in Veritases, Theo Fitzau and Gunther Bechem in A.F.M.s, Edgar Barth in an E.M.W., and Ernst Klodwig in a B.M.W. Ahead of all these on the grid were numerous Gordinis, Cooper-Bristols, Connaughts and Stirling Moss' second and more competitive Cooper-Alta. At the start Fangio grabbed an initial lead but was soon overtaken by Ascari who then built up an appreciable cushion between himself and Fangio, Hawthorn and Farina. Hawthorn overtook Fangio and the two remained in close combat. Ascari steadily increased his lead by 10 seconds a lap until he drove slowly round to the pits with only three wheels! It took 4 minutes 12 seconds to get him started again as he had overshot his pit by a wide margin rather than risk using his brakes to stop. The order became Hawthorn, Fangio, Farina, Villoresi with Farina joining the leading pair and the three drawing away from the rest of the field. Ascari took over Villoresi's Ferrari but overcooked his engine in the process of trying to catch the leaders. So the race went to Farina's Ferrari at 83.91mph, with Fangio's Maserati second and Hawthorn's Ferrari third. Stirling Moss was the first British finisher, coming home in sixth place. The fastest lap went to Ascari at 85.61mph.

The Swiss Grand Prix. Berne: August 23

Juan Fangio's Maserati was fastest in practice at Berne and had the Ferraris of Alberto Ascari and Giuseppe Farina next to it on the starting grid. Maurice Trintignant's Gordini was on the second grid alongside Onofre Marimon's Maserati. Then came Luigi Villoresi, Mike Hawthorn and Toulo de Graffenried. Back in eleventh place was the great Hermann Lang who had been invited to take the place of Froilan Gonzales, who had still not fully recovered from his accident, in a Maserati. Three H.W.M.s were driven by Lance Macklin, Paul Frere and Albert Scherrer. First Fangio and then Ascari led in the course of the first lap and behind them were Hawthorn, Marimon, Villoresi, Bonetto and Farina. Then Ascari established a commanding lead over Fangio whose car developed gearbox problems and eventually Fangio switched cars with Bonetto. Finally he was out of the race in a cloud of smoke on lap 29 with a blown engine. Having enjoyed a substantial lead Ascari was delayed by having to stop to have a carburettor jet cleared, and he then proceeded to put on a display of his superb mastery to the delight of the crowd by chasing, catching and passing Farina, Marimon and Hawthorn to win at an average speed of 97.160mph. Lang finished in fifth place, three laps behind the winner. Wharton was 7th in a his Cooper Bristol and Albert Scherrer, driving in his only Grand Prix, ninth in an H.W.M. Ascari recorded the fastest lap of the race at 100.961mph.

The Italian Grand Prix. Monza: September 13

Alberto Ascari leading Onofre Marimon during the Italian Grand Prix.

The Spanish Grand Prix which was due to take place on October 26 was cancelled and so the race at Monza would be the last of the season. It was of course the race which Maserati most dearly wanted to win but Enzo Ferrari had no wish to see this happen and produced two new Tipo 553 Super Squalo cars with space frames and shorter wheelbases which, however, proved to be no faster than the previous model. More would be seen of them in 1954. The grid formation consisted of ten rows of three cars and the order was Alberto Ascari (Ferrari), Juan Fangio (Maserati) and Giuseppe Farina (Ferrari) in the front row and Onofre Marimon (Maserati), Luigi Villoresi (Ferrari) and Mike Hawthorn (Ferrari) immediately behind. Umberto Maglioli had one of the new Ferraris, whereas Ascari, Farina and Marimon chose the well tried models. Sergio Mantovani drove the third works Maserati. Further back there was Stirling Moss' Cooper-Alta, the Connaughts of Roy Salvadori, Kenneth McAlpine and Jack Fairman, the H.W.M.s of Lance Macklin, John Fitch and Philippe Giraud-Cabantous and the Cooper-Bristols of Ken Wharton and Alan Brown. It was again Ascari who led away from the grid with Farina and Marimon in second and third places, but Marimon snatched the lead before the end of the first lap followed by Ascari, Farina, Fangio, and Moss who discovered that his fuel injected Cooper Alta had enough power to stay with the Italian cars. Sadly Moss had to call at his pit to check an oil leak and was eventually delayed by tyre trouble and a split fuel tank. The three leading cars constantly swopped positions while Villoresi, Hawthorn and Trintignant were similarly engaged further back. Marimon dropped out of contention on lap 46 but when Ascari, Farina and Fangio lapped the second group of Italian cars the six travelled at top speed and in close company. On the very last bend of the race Ascari, who was alongside Farina, spun on a patch of oil and his car was struck by Marimon's Maserati. Fangio won at an average speed of 110.685mph and so Maserati had achieved its first win of the year in the race that mattered most. Farina, Villoresi and Hawthorn came second, third and fourth. Brown and Moss were twelfth and thirteenth in their cars from Surbiton. Fangio also set the fastest lap of the race at 113.194mph.

The World Championship

Alberto Ascari won the 1953 World Championship decisively with 34½ points, Juan Fangio came second with 28, Giuseppe Farina third with 26, Mike Hawthorn fourth with 19, Luigi Villoresi fifth with 17 and Froilan Gonzales sixth with 13½.

Monte Carlo Rally

Of 1000 applicants a record number of 404 cars started the Monte Carlo Rally of which 112 started from Glasgow. The large number of manufacturers represented included A.C.,

Juan Fangio in his B.R.M. before the start of the Woodcote Cup Race at Goodwood.

Fangio running in second place during the Formula Libre Race at Silverstone on July 18 1953.

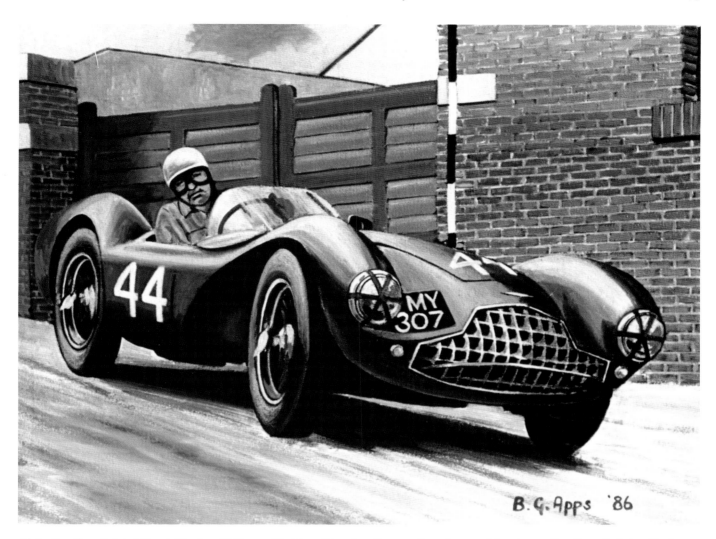

B.G. Apps '86

Alvis, Bentley, Bristol, Ford, Healey, Hillman, Holden, Humber, Jensen, Lanchester, Morris, Porsche, Rover, Riley, Singer, Standard, Sunbeam Talbot, Triumph, Volkswagen, and Wolseley, and there was plenty for the groups who gathered at points along the route to see. Notable amongst the entrants was Stirling Moss, Geoff Imhoff and Raymond Baxter in Sunbeam Talbots and the previous year's winners, Sydney Allard and P. Worledge once

Reg Parnell's Aston Martin DB3S winning the British Empire Trophy Race in Douglas, Isle of Man.

Mike Hawthorn winning the Goodwood Trophy Race in the Thin Wall Special Ferrari on September 26.

again in an Allard saloon. One car was equipped with sand to be poured in front of its wheels to give added traction. The conditions were comparatively mild and this resulted in 356 cars reaching Monte Carlo. Of these, 253 had clean sheets. Sydney Allard was fastest in the accelerating, braking and reversing test over 250 metres, but the winners were Maurice Gatsonides and P. Worledge in a Ford Zephyr. The Appleyards came second in a Mark VII Jaguar and a Citroen driven by Marion and Charmasson was third. A Panhard Dyna driven by Grosgogeat and Biagini was fourth and Vard and Jolley's Mark V Jaguar fifth.

The Alfa Romeo with which Juan Fangio finished in second place in the Mille Miglia.

Mille Miglia

In 1953 the Mille Miglia was one of seven events which qualified for the new annual World Sports Car Championship. In the absence of Mercedes Benz, Alfa Romeo produced three 6C - 3000 cars for Fangio, Kling and Senesi, Lancia had new D20s for Taruffi, Biondetti, Magliolo, and Bonetto, and Ferrari entered 4.1 litre spiders with bodies by Touring cars for Bracco, Villoresi, Farina, Hawthorn and the Marzotto brothers. Jaguar brought along a team of C Types, determined to put in a good effort. In *All My Races*, Stirling Moss records how he covered 6000 miles on the course during the fortnight before the race but, sadly, retired before Ravenna with transmission problems. It was Jaguar's last Mille Miglia. There were three Aston Martin DB3s for Parnell, Abecassis and Collins and they also arrived early enough to practice extensively before the race. For once the conditions were fine

Stirling Moss with Mort Morris-Goodall driving through Brescia at speed in his C Type Jaguar during the 1953 Mille Miglia.

and it was Sanesi who established an early lead and held it all the way to Pescara, followed by Farina, Kling and Fangio. Then Sanesi, Farina, Kling and Villoresi were all eliminated through accidents or mechanical problems and it was Fangio who led until failing brakes and a fault in the steering mechanism enabled Marzotto to win. Collins crashed into the

parapet of a bridge near Siena but Parnell finished 5th with a time of 11 hours, 32 minutes and 43 seconds, the highest place that a British car ever achieved in the Mille Miglia.

Le Mans

Jaguar returned to Le Mans determined to make amends for its disastrous showing the previous year. The team of C Types looked much as they had done in 1951 and no last minute scares were anticipated.

Luigi Villoresi's Ferrari leading the D Type Jaguars of Stirling Moss and Tony Rolt at Le Mans in 1953.

Duncan Hamilton's C Type being pursued by Alberto Ascari's Ferrari at Le Mans.

1953 promised to be a vintage year at Le Mans with a team of V8 2.6 litre Lancias with space frames and independent suspension on all four wheels driven by Taruffi/ Maglioli, Manzon/ Chiron, Bonetto/Valenzano and Gonzales/Biondetti. The team of Alfa Romeo Coupes were driven by Sanesi/ Carini, Fangio/ Marimon and Kling/ Riess. There was a 4.5 litre Ferrari for Ascari/Villoresi and two 4.1 litre models for Farina/Hawthorn and Paulo/Marzotto. In addition there was a new team of Bristol Coupes, based on the G Type E.R.A. and with futuristic bodies which incorporated tail fins. The works Jaguars were driven by Moss/Walker, Rolt/Hamilton and Whitehead/Stewart. There were three Aston Martin DB3S cars driven by Parnell/Collins, Salvadori/Abecassis and Poore/Thompson and a supercharged DB2 driven by Clark/Meyer. Two Austin Healey 100s were driven by Becquart/Wilkins and Gatsonides/Lockett. The Rolt/Hamilton Jaguar was disqualified when another car with the same number was practising at the same time. However the matter was sorted out at the last minute and it was allowed to start after all.

It was Sydney Allard who led at the start in one of his own cars but soon Moss and Villoresi were at the head of the pack. Eventually the Rolt/Hamilton Jaguar came through to lead the Ferrari of Ascari/Villoresi and what was described by *Motor Sport* as 'the fiercest battle ever fought on the Sarthe circuit' began. It raged all through the night, Hamilton, disclosing afterwards that he regarded the hours of darkness as an opportunity to really press on. He broke the lap record in the dark while the Ferrari gradually lost ground. All the Lancias retired but the two Alfa Romeos of Kling/Riess and Sanesi/Carini took up the chase behind the leading Jaguar. These also succumbed in time and the result was that the Rolt/Hamilton car won and the C Type of Moss/Walker came second. Whitehead/Stewart were fourth and a privately entered C Type driven by Laurent/de Tornaco was placed ninth. A 5.4 litre Cunningham driven by Walters/Cunningham was third and the 4.1 litre

A signed painting of Duncan Hamilton winning the Le Mans 24 Hour race.

The CR5 Cunningham on its way to third place at Le Mans in 1953.

The Fitch/Walters Cunningham C4-R winning the Sebring 12 Hours Race in 1953.

Ferrari of P. and G. Marzotto fifth. Of the three Aston Martin DB3Ss the Parnell/Collins car was eliminated during the second hour due to a crash, the Salvadori/Abecassis car retired with clutch failure during the tenth hour, and the Aston of Poore/Thompson retired in the eighteenth hour with engine trouble. The Aston Martin DB2 driven by Clark/Meyer, retired in the first hour.

1954
A display of Teutonic thoroughness

Piero Taruffi

FORMULA 2 HAD proved to be an excellent stop-gap before the new Formula for 2.5 litre unsupercharged cars came in at the beginning of 1954. Inevitably the 2 litre cars had lacked the presence of the Alfa Romeos, Ferraris and Lago Talbots of earlier years but the Ferraris and Maseratis were evenly matched and, in the hands of such masters as Ascari and Fangio, they had produced many exciting races, the most memorable being the dual between Fangio and Hawthorn at Rheims in 1953. So the prospect of seeing more powerful and entirely new 2.5 litre cars with the introduction of the new Formula was eagerly anticipated. The most notable development in 1954 was the return of Mercedes Benz after the war, led by its legendary Team Manager Alfred Neubauer. The W196 had a straight 8 engine with fuel injection and desmodromic valves. It had a stressed tubular frame and inboard drum brakes. Sensationally it had a fully streamlined body which was to prove ideal on the fast Rheims circuit but quite unsuitable for Silverstone where its drivers would be unable to see the oil drums that defined the track. Nothing if not thorough, Mercedes rapidly provided a solution to this problem with its more conventional open-wheeled car. Maserati produced its famous 6 cylinder 250F for the new Formula with a 6 cylinder engine, coil front springs and a De Dion tube at the back. Ferrari were to struggle with its Super Squalo cars which first appeared at the end of 1953 in 2 litre form and so resorted to the well tried Tipo 500 with an enlarged engine. Much excitement was generated by the arrival of the entirely new V8 Lancia D50 designed by Vittorio Jano of Alfa Romeo fame. An innovative feature was the use of its engine to support the rigidity of the chassis and the front suspension. Its most distinguishing attributes were its pannier fuel tanks which were positioned between the front and back wheels on each side, enabling the weight of its fuel load to remain evenly distributed throughout the course of a race. They would eventually be discarded when the cars were progressively developed as Lancia-Ferraris. France was again represented by the faithful old Gordinis with suitably enlarged engines. Britain had the H.W.M.s with their engines enlarged to 2.5 litres, and Connaught had developed 2.5 Alta engines adopting fuel injection in their B Types with the assistance of Weslake. Tony Vandervell had a car specially designed by

Cooper, powered by his own 2 litre engine based on four single cylinder Norton engines and called the Vanwall Special. B.R.M. had an entirely new 4 cylinder car in preparation but, in the meantime raced a 250F Maserati which, with Dunlop disc brakes and alloy wheels, was known as the Owen Maserati.

THE WORLD CHAMPIONSHIP SEASON
The Argentine Grand Prix. Buenos Aires: January 17

In the absence of both Mercedes Benz and Lancia the opening race of the new Season at Buenos Aires saw a return of the 'old firms'. Both Alberto Ascari and Luigi Villoresi had signed contracts with Lancia and Fangio was committed to Mercedes Benz, but Juan Fangio was allowed to race for Maserati in Argentina and he was third in practice with the Ferraris of Giuseppe Farina, Froilan Gonzales and Mike Hawthorn first, second and fourth on the front row of the starting grid. Ferraris and Maseratis filled the first fourteen places, Prince Bira's Maserati being 9th and Toulo de Graffenried's 12th. Farina took an immediate lead followed by Fangio, Hawthorn and Gonzales, but Gonzales overtook first Hawthorn and then both Fangio and Farina to lead the race by lap 15. After this Gonzales spun in heavy rain and lost several places and Farina stopped to exchange his goggles for a visor. Fangio, superlative as always in the rain, regained the lead and Hawthorn spun in the appalling conditions. On lap 61 Fangio came in for rain tyres and, after the Ferrari pit had complained that more than the permitted number of mechanics had carried out the operation, the Ferraris eased back mistakenly believing that he would be disqualified. Such was not the case and Fangio overtook Farina and Gonzales to win the race. The order at the end was Fangio, Farina, Gonzales and Maurice Trintignant. Fangio's average speed was 70.130mph but the fastest lap was registered by Gonzales at 80.763mph.

The Belgian Grand Prix. Spa: June 20

In the continued absence of the Mercedes Benz and Lancia teams the Ferraris and Maseratis returned to do battle at Spa. Fangio, on loan again from Mercedes Benz, was there to deny Ferrari the advantage of monopolising the front row which consisted of Fangio on pole in a 250F Maserati and both Farina and Gonzales in Super Squalo Ferraris. Farina had said that he preferred the older model which was Hawthorn's mount in the second row, where he was alongside Onofre Marimon. Three Gordinis were present in the hands of Andre Pilette, Jean Behra and Paul Frere. Stirling Moss was in the fourth row with his own 250F Maserati, Alfred Neubauer having advised him to gain experience with a more competitive car. Gonzales led away from the start in his Super Squalo Ferrari, followed by Fangio, Farina and Hawthorn. After Hawthorn came Marimon's Maserati, Pilette's Gordini, Trintignant's Ferrari and Behra's Gordini. Roberto Mieres' Maserati caught fire after fuel spilt out of its tank and he jumped out without waiting for it to stop. At the end of the lap the Ferraris of Gonzales and the Belgian Jacques Swaters were out and it was Fangio who led from Farina and Hawthorn, but Fangio came into his pit on lap 11 to remove his visor which had a broken strap. Three laps later he was in the lead again while Hawthorn slowed as he was suffering from fumes from a split exhaust pipe. Soon after losing the lead to Fangio, Farina retired with electrical problems. Hawthorn came into his pits barely conscious and therefore unable to explain the cause. Gonzales immediately took his place, only to discover for himself the problem with the exhaust and stopped for quick repairs. So the race went to Fangio by a large margin with Trintignant in second place with a 1953 Ferrari and Stirling Moss, who was nursing a car with low oil pressure, third. The Hawthorn/Gonzales Ferrari finished fourth, having recovered two places after the car's second pit stop. It seemed that in Fangio's hands the 250F Maserati had the advantage and that the new Super Squalos had yet to prove themselves.

The new streamlined W196 Mercedes Benz of Karl Kling and Juan Fangio leading at the start of the French Grand Prix.

The French Grand Prix. Rheims: July 4

The French Grand Prix at Rheims saw the return of Mercedes Benz to Grand Prix motor racing and the debut of the beautifully streamlined W196 in the hands of Juan Fangio, Karl Kling and Hans Herrmann. Their arrival had been eagerly awaited and they did not disappoint. During practice the new cars had a tendency to cut out momentarily on the long straights of Rheims but this was dismissed as being merely due to the fuel mixture, and Fangio and Kling were first and second in practice with Hermann back in 7th place on the grid. It has to be added that Alberto Ascari, loaned by Lancia to drive a Ferrari, was a mere 0.1 seconds slower than Kling and one wondered how the Italian master would have performed against the Mercedes team had he been driving a new Lancia D50. The high speed circuit undoubtedly favoured the wind cheating lines of the Mercedes and, from the start of the race, Fangio and Kling established an immediate lead, while disappointingly Ascari made a slow start due to a transmission problem and pulled out at the end of the first lap. Froilan Gonzales managed to hold on to the two Mercedes at first but spun on lap 13. The order after the two leading W196s was Mike Hawthorn, Onofre Marimon, Prince Bira and Roberto Mieres, but Herrmann gained in confidence and steadily climbed up the field so that the three Mercedes assumed the first three places. In the process of achieving this Herrmann established a new lap record but then his car expired in a cloud of smoke on lap 17. Any hopes that the new Mercedes would prove to be fragile were unjustified and with the Italian challenge having faded, Bira's Maserati in third place being half a lap behind, the two leading cars motored side by side with Kling even having time to scratch his nose! Ascari, Gonzales and Hawthorn were all out and it was merely a question of who would be

Fangio at speed during the French Grand Prix at Rheims.

the best of the rest. Behind Bira there was Trintignant's Ferrari, Manzon's Ferrari, Villoresi's Maserati, and Frere's Gordini. Trintignant managed to overtake Bira towards the end but was then himself overtaken as his car ran out of fuel. The Mercedes of Fangio finished first with Kling only 0.1 of a second behind him. Manzon was third one lap behind, Bira fourth, Villoresi fifth, and the Gordinis of Behra and Frere sixth and seventh. Ken Wharton drove the Owen Maserati and, after being 16th in practice, retired with transmission trouble on lap 20. Fangio's winning average speed was 115.971mph. Herrmann's new record lap stood at 121.455mph. The performance of the new Mercedes prompted Motor Sport to comment that it represented 'a new era of science versus the rest'.

The British Grand Prix. Silverstone: July 17

Silverstone was a very different venue from Rheims and it might have been expected that the Italian cars would more evenly match the new W196 Mercedes Benz from Stuttgart in their second encounter. Stirling Moss had his own green 250F Maserati which had been prepared by his mechanic Alf Francis in Modena. He was fourth fastest in practice and on the front row of the grid alongside Mike Hawthorn. Predictably Juan Fangio was in pole position with his Mercedes but it was the Ferrari of Froilan Gonzales who was in second spot and Karl Kling was only on the second row, 6th in practice. Peter Collins had the new 2.3 litre Vanwall Special, which had been designed by Cooper and is not to be confused with the later Colin Chapman cars, in 11th place. Connaughts, Cooper-Bristols and Cooper-Altas mingled with Gordinis further down the grid but, sadly, no longer any H.W.M.s.

Starting Grid

S. Moss	J.M. Hawthorn	J.F. Gonzales	J.M. Fangio
Maserati	Ferrari	Ferrari	Mercedes Benz
1 min 47 secs	1 min 46 secs	1 min 46 secs	1 min 45 secs

R. Salvadori	K. Kling	J.Behra
Maserati	Mercedes Benz	Gordini
1 min 48 secs	1 min 48 secs	1 min 48 secs

P. Collins	B. Bira	K. Wharton	M. Trintignant
Vanwall Special	Maserati	Maserati	Ferrari
1 min 50 secs	1 min 49 secs	1 min 49 secs	1 min 48 secs

R. Parnell	C. Bucci	A. Pilette
Ferrari	Gordini	Gordini
I min 52 secs	1 min 52 secs	1 min 51 secs

F. R. Gerard	D. Beauman	H. Schell	R. Manzon
Cooper-Bristol	Connaught	Maserati	Ferrari
1 min 55 secs	1 min 55 secs	1 min 53 secs	1 min 52 secs

J. Riseley- Prichard	H. Gould	W. Whitehouse
Connaught	Cooper-Bristol	Connaught
1 min 58 secs	1 min 56 secs	1 min 56 secs

E. Brandon	P. Whitehead	L. Thorne	L. Marr
Cooper- Bristol	Cooper-Alta	Connaught	Connaught
2 min 05 secs	2 mins	1 min 59 secs	1 min 58 secs

O. Marimon	L. Villoresi	A. Brown *
Maserati	Maserati	Cooper-Bristol

R. Mieres	A. Ascari	L. Rosier
Maserati	Maserati	Ferrari

*The last six cars on the grid arrived too late for practice.**

As the race got underway on the Saturday afternoon it soon became apparent that the Mercedes Benz drivers were severely handicapped by their inability to see the tops of the oil drums which lined the circuit over the front wheel fairings of their cars. It resulted in bent metal and lost time as they began to strike them. Gonzales led at the start with his slim 1953 car equipped with the latest engine and Fangio soon overtook Hawthorn to run in second place about 5 seconds behind the flying Gonzales. Moss caught up with Hawthorn and eventually overtook him to establish a secure third place for himself. The Vanwall Special retired with a blown gasket and Alberto Ascari, who had started from the back of the grid having failed to establish a time during practice in his works Maserati, went out with a bent valve. Ascari exchanged places with Luigi Villoresi, who was also waiting for his new Lancia, but this car also failed on lap 41. In the meantime Fangio was regularly colliding with the oil drums and he also lost third gear so that he fell back behind Moss, Hawthorn

Froilan Gonzales driving the new Type 553 Squalo Ferrari in the rain during the International Trophy Race at Silverstone on May 7 1954.

Jean Behra's Gordini during the British Grand Prix.

Luigi Villoresi suffering the result of a broken connecting rod at Silverstone.

and Onofre Marimon. Moss was cruelly robbed of second place when his rear axle failed. The result was a convincing win by Gonzales who was never challenged and who had thrown his car around with broad slides in the rain, enjoying himself immensely. Hawthorn's Ferrari came second and Marimon third in his Maserati. The first British car to finish was the immaculately prepared Cooper-Bristol of Bob Gerard. Moss shared the fastest lap of the race with Gonzales, Hawthorn, Marimon, Fangio, Jean Behra and Ascari. Perhaps it was too early to speak of the dominance of the W196 after all! The 'Owen' Maserati finished eighth in Ken Wharton's hands. The winner's average speed was 89.69mph and the speed of the fastest lap of the race was 95.79mph.

Results

1. J.F. Gonzales Ferrari 2 hrs 56 mins 14 secs.
2. J.M. Hawthorn Ferrari 2 hrs 57 mins 24 secs
3. O. Marimon Maserati 1 lap behind
4. J.M. Fangio Mercedes Benz
5. M. Trintignant Ferrari 3 laps behind
6. R. Mieres Maserati
7. K. Kling Mercedes Benz
8. K. Wharton Maserati 4 laps behind
9. A. Pilette Gordini
10. F.R. Gerard Cooper-Bristol 5 laps behind
11. D. Beauman Connaught 6 laps behind
12. H. Schell Maserati 7 laps behind
13. L. Marr Connaught 8 laps behind
14. L. Thorne Connaught 12 laps behind
15. H. Gould Cooper-Bristol 46 laps behind.

Retirements: E. Brandon Cooper-Bristol engine on lap 3, L. Rosier Ferrari engine trouble on lap 3, P. Whitehead Cooper-Alta fractured oil pipe on lap 5, R. Manzon Ferrari cracked cylinder block on lap 16, P. Collins Vanwall Special blown gasket on lap 17, C. Bucci Gordini crash on lap 18, A. Ascari Maserati bent valve on lap 21, R. Parnell Ferrari engine failure on lap 26, L. Villoresi/A. Ascari Maserati engine failure on lap 41, J. Riseley Pritchard Connaught crash on lap 41, B. Bira/R. Flockhart Maserati crash on lap 45, R. Salvadori Maserati transmission failure on lap 54, J. Behra Gordini suspension failure on lap 55, W. Whitehouse Connaught engine failure on lap 64, S. Moss Maserati rear axle failure on lap 80.

The Aston Martin team took the first three places in the Sports Car race, led by Peter Collins. Archie Scott Brown won the 1½ - 2 litre Class in his Lister Jaguar and Parnell the over 3 litre Class in a Lagonda.

The German Grand Prix. Nurburgring: August 1

It was important for Mercedes Benz to win at the Nurburgring and Hermann Lang, the 1939 European Champion, was invited to drive a fourth car. Following their Silverstone experience Juan Fangio, Karl Kling and Lang were provided with open wheeled cars which

A photograph, signed by George Monkhouse, of Onofre Marimon the lap before he was killed during practice for the 1954 German Grand Prix.

George Monkhouse described as having 'rather flat wide bodies, a gaping maw for a radiator intake, and exposed wheels'. Even less flattering *Motor Sport* described them as 'gormless looking single seaters of vast width'. Hans Herrmann had to cope with the Streamliner. Sadly, Onofre Marimon was killed in practice when his Maserati crashed and the official Maserati team was withdrawn from the race as a sign of respect. Fangio gained pole position but had Mike Hawthorn and Stirling Moss alongside him on the front row. Stirling's Maserati had been hurriedly painted red with a green band around its nose as it had been given works patronage. Herrmann was third and on the second row with Froilan Gonzales, who was devastated by the loss of his friend and compatriot, and Lang could do no better than 11th. Giuseppe Farina was still absent following his accident earlier in the year and Piero Taruffi was drafted in to take his place in the Ferrari team. A record crowd of 300 000 had come to watch Mercedes Benz win and by the end of the first lap Fangio led from Gonzales, having overtaken him soon after the start. Moss, Lang, Herrmann and Hawthorn followed Gonzales, and Kling had climbed to 10th place from the back of the grid. By lap four Lang was third and Kling fourth as Moss had dropped out of third position on lap 2 with a blown engine and Hawthorn's Ferrari had retired with a broken rear axle. Herrmann's

Mercedes retired on lap 8 with fuel leaking from a broken pipe, and Gonzales dropped back, his heart not in the race. Lang spun and stopped on lap 11, and Kling, ignoring the team orders for both of them to ease back, overtook Fangio to lead the race on lap 15. His suspension broke one lap later and he had to come into the pits for repairs before rejoining the race at a reduced speed after a severe ticking off. Gonzales' car was given to Hawthorn, but Fangio continued on his serene way to win the race from the Ferraris of Gonzales/ Hawthorn and Trintignant. Herrmann managed to cling on to fourth place, followed by Sergio Mantovani (Maserati), Piero Taruffi (Ferrari), Harry Schell ((Maserati), Louis Rosier (Ferrari), Robert Manzon (Ferrari), and Jean Behra (Gordini). Fangio's average speed was 82.87mph. The fastest lap was recorded by Kling at 85.74mph.

The Swiss Grand Prix. Berne: August 22

Froilan Gonzales managed to put the death of Onofre Marimon behind him at Berne and posted the fastest lap in practice with his 1953/4 Ferrari in what would prove to be the last Swiss Grand Prix of all. Next to Gonzales came Juan Fangio in the open wheeled Mercedes

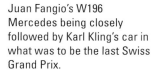

Juan Fangio's W196 Mercedes being closely followed by Karl Kling's car in what was to be the last Swiss Grand Prix.

and Stirling Moss in his red works supported Maserati. Fourth was Maurice Trintignant's 1953 Ferrari with updated engine, while Karl Kling was fifth and Hans Herrmann seventh. Harry Schell's Maserati had a right hand accelerator so that it could be used as a reserve car for Moss. Ken Wharton's Owen Maserati, with its Dunlop disc brakes and alloy wheels, was eighth. A 1954 Super Squalo was allotted to Umberto Maglioli. At the start Fangio led Gonzales, Moss and Kling but Kling then dropped to last place after a spin and Moss passed Gonzales to run second to Fangio on lap 3. While Fangio continued to stretch his lead, Mike Hawthorn moved up to fourth position and made rapid progress, passing first Gonzales and then Moss. Soon afterwards, Moss retired on lap 22 with low oil pressure. Hawthorn dropped out on lap 31 with fuel pump failure and Kling, having recovered from his early spin moved up to third place behind Fangio and Gonzales. Then Kling retired on lap 39 with fuel starvation. So the race was won by Fangio from Gonzales with Herrmann in third place. Then came the Maseratis of Roberto Mieres, Sergio Mantovani and Ken Wharton, and the Ferraris of Maglioli and Jacques Swaters. The race was won at an average speed of 99.202mph by Fangio who also set the fastest lap of the race at 101.972mph.

The Italian Grand Prix. Monza: September 5

As had been the case in 1953, the starting grid at Monza consisted of lines of three cars and at the front were the Mercedes Benz, Ferrari and Maserati of Juan Fangio, Alberto Ascari and Stirling Moss. Fangio had the streamlined car for this fast circuit and Moss' Maserati, now fully under the umbrella of the works, was equipped with a works engine and, like the works cars, a tail mounted oil tank. Karl Kling was fourth with another streamlined Mercedes while Hans Herrmann was back in eighth place. At the start of the race Kling came through from the second row to lead Fangio by the closest of margins and they were closely followed by Ascari, Froilan Gonzales, Moss and Herrmann. Kling was then relegated to fifth place after running wide on lap 5 and the order of the tightly packed field then became Ascari, Gonzales, Fangio and Moss. Herrmann slowed and stopped for new plugs and Gonzales, having dropped out with gearbox problems, took over Umberto Maglioli's car and started to move up the field. By lap 10 Ascari had a 6 second lead but then Fangio speeded up and drew level with him. Kling, blinded by his own oil, crashed at Lesmo and retired while Luigi Villoresi, loaned by Maserati from Lancia, overtook Moss, Ascari and Fangio to lead the race on lap 41. Two laps later Villoresi's clutch disintegrated and it was Moss who led. They lapped Hawthorn and Ascari took the lead from Moss on lap 45 only to pull out of the race with a broken valve four laps later. By lap 60 Moss had established a lead of 15 seconds and looked an assured winner, but he had to pit briefly to replenish the oil in his split tank and then stopped less than a lap later with his engine dry of oil. This allowed Fangio to cross the line and to win the race with an engine which sounded distinctly sick. Hawthorn was fortunate to inherit second place, Maglioli/Gonzales Ferrari was third and Herrmann's Mercedes Benz fourth. Fangio's winning speed was 111.982mph. Gonzales achieved the fastest lap of the race at 116.661mph.

Mike Hawthorn's Tipo 625 Ferrari during the 1954 Italian Grand Prix.

The Spanish Grand Prix. Barcelona: October 24

The long awaited Lancias were at last present at the Pedralbes circuit outside Barcelona for the Spanish Grand Prix and Alberto Ascari established the fastest time in practice. With him on the front line was Juan Fangio's open wheeled W196, Mike Hawthorn's Super Squalo Ferrari, which had been fitted with coil springs in the front, and Harry Schell's Maserati. Luigi Villoresi, in the second Lancia, was next up on the second row of the grid accompanied by Stirling Moss, who had crashed one Maserati in practice, and Luigi Musso. Hans Herrmann and Karl Kling were 9th and 12th on the grid. Peter Collins crashed the 2.5 litre Vanwall in practice and so was unable to take part in the race. Schell, with a light fuel load took the lead at the start of the race and he was followed by Hawthorn, Ascari, Maurice Trinignant, Moss, Fangio, Herrmann and Villoresi. Disappointingly Villoresi's Lancia retired with brake trouble on lap 2, but Ascari passed Schell and Hawthorn on lap 3 to lead the race and he proceeded to draw away from them. However Ascari was in the pits after nine laps and, following a brief stay, retired on the following lap with an inoperable clutch. Lancia's day was over but Ascari had clearly demonstrated the potential of the D50. Moss retired on lap 20 with an oil pump failure and Herrmann on lap 51 with a faulty fuel injection pump. Hawthorn's Super Squalo Ferrari led Fangio by 20 seconds but hot oil was spraying upon Fangio's arm and so Luigi Musso's Maserati was able to pass the slowing Mercedes. So Hawthorn won the race at 97.169mph from Musso and Fangio but the fastest lap of the race was achieved by Ascari at 100.629mph. Roberto Mieres was fourth in a Maserati, Kling fifth, and then Maseratis followed, in the order of Francisco Godia, Louis Rosier, Ken Wharton and Prince Bira.

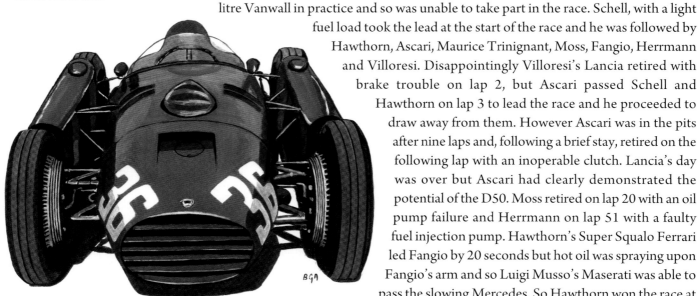

The Lancia D50 as it appeared at Barcelona for the Spanish Grand Prix in 1954.

The season had not ended as Mercedes Benz team would have wished and the W196 failed to maintained the dominance it had displayed originally at Rheims. The new Lancias offered an exciting prospect for 1955 and the cars from Stuttgart could be relied upon to come back strongly. With four different makes of cars on the front row of the starting grid in Spain the new Formula was proving to be a resounding success.

The World Championship

Juan Fangio won the World Championship in 1954 with 42 points and was followed by three Ferrari drivers. Froilan Gonzales was second with 25½ points, Mike Hawthorn third with 24 9/14 points and Maurice Trintignant fourth with 17 points. Karl Kling and Hans Herrmann came 5th and 7th. Stirling Moss was only 13th in spite of his fine performances and Ascari's efforts with Maserati, Ferrari and Lancia resulted in only 1½ points.

Monte Carlo Rally

The weather was kind to the competitors in 1954, although Imhof's drive in a Humber Super Snipe ended when it skidded on ice into a ditch. As most of the competitors reached Monte Carlo everything depended on the Regularity Test of 164 miles on the Maritime Alps and the competition on the famous Monaco Grand Prix road circuit. After leading the Rally, Adams and Titterington came sixth in a Jaguar and they were the highest of the British contingent. Stirling Moss was fastest of all comers in the Regularity Section in his Sunbeam Talbot. The popular winner was Louis Chiron with Ciro Basadonna in a 2.5 litre Lancia Aurelia. Second was the 1.3 litre Peugeot of David and Barbier. The little 750cc Panhard of

Ken Wharton's V16 B.R.M. inches ahead of Roy Salvadori's 250F Maserati during the Glover Trophy Race at Goodwood in 1954.

Stirling Moss about to overtake Reg Parnell to win the Oulton Park Gold Cup.

Alan Brown driving the first Vanwall Special in the International Trophy Race at Silverstone.

Peter Collins driving the 4.5 litre V12 Thin Wall Special in a very wet Aintree in 1954.

John Easton Gibson's Daimler boarding the *Lord Warden* at Dover during the 1954 Monte Carlo Rally.

Blanchard and Lecoq came third. Another Jaguar was 8th, two Ford Zephyrs 13th and 14th and the Moss/Scannell Sunbeam Talbot 15th.

The Mille Miglia

Four new V6 3.3 litre D24 Lancias with open 2 seater bodies by Pinin Farina came to compete in the 1954 Mille Miglia to be driven by Taruffi, Ascari, Castellotti and Valenzano. They drove alone with covers over the passenger seats. Piodi and Anselmi had 2.5 litre Lancia Aurelias. Against them was ranged a team of V12 4.9 litre Ferraris for Farina, Maglioli, Giannino Marzotto and Paulo Marzotto. Scotti had a 4.5 litre Ferrari and Biondetti a 3 litre car. There were two Aston Martin DB3S cars for Parnell and Collins, John Wyer believing that the outstanding road holding of his cars on the mountain roads would compensate for their lack of power. Abecassis had a Jaguar engined H.W.M., and there was a team of Austin Healeys. The route passed through Mantua as a tribute to the great Tazio Nuvolari who had died the previous August.

The race was accompanied by fog and rain, the first car being starting at 9 0 p.m. on Saturday evening and the last at 6.13 a.m. the following morning. Taruffi made the running in the early stages, averaging 109mph, and he was followed by Ascari, Castellotti and Maglioli. Parnell's DB3S was in sixth place at Pescara but came to grief when he ran into the debris of a crashing car. Collins lay in fifth place for much of the race but ploughed 50 ft down a mountain side when a tyre burst, and he was retired by John Wyer at Florence for reasons of safety. Then both Taruffi and Castellotti retired near Rome and it was

Luigi Musso's A6GCS Maserati between Florence and Bologna during the 1954 Mille Miglia.

Ascari's Lancia D24 closing up on Claes's Cisitalia to win the 1954 Mille Miglia at 87.27mph.

Ascari at the front. Ascari eventually emerged as the clear winner, his first in the Mille Miglia. Vittorio Marzotto was second in a Ferrari, Musso third in a Maserati and Biondetti fourth in another Ferrari.

Le Mans

There were no Lancias at Le Mans in 1954 but there were three 4.9 litre Ferraris for Gonzales/Trintignant, Rosier/Manzon and Marzotto/Maglioli and these were ranged against the D Type Jaguars of Moss/Walker, Rolt/Hamilton and Whitehead/Wharton. David Brown put everything that he had got into the race with a 4.5 litre Lagonda, which looked remarkably like a large DB3S driven by Poore/Thompson, a supercharged 2.9 DB3S for Parnell/Salvadori, two coupe models for Bira/Collins and Graham Whitehead/Jimmy Stewart and one painted white and blue for Shelby/Frere. *Motor Sport* gave the race a great coverage and described it as a battle between brute force and science, adding that it produced the closest finish since early 1930s.

The Ferraris of Gonzales, Manzon and Marzotto led Moss, Rolt and Wharton initially but at 8pm the supercharged Aston Martin was lying in 5th place with Hamilton 6th. Stewart's Aston Martin overturned at about 10pm, the driver sustaining a broken arm, and Maglioli's Ferrari stopped two hours later with gearbox trouble. Whitehead also retired with a similar problem. The race then developed into a high speed chase in heavy rain with the Rolt/Hamilton Jaguar catching the Gonzales/Trintignant Ferrari. When the rain stopped Gonzales was able to increase his lead and Rolt was forced to leave the circuit temporarily in avoiding a slower car. Rain returned and, with one hour to go, Hamilton was only 1 minute 36 seconds behind the big Ferrari. It proved just too much in drying conditions and

The 2 litre Bristols at Le Mans in 1954. No 35, driven by Wilson/Mayers, finished in 7th place and No 34, driven by Keen/Line, came 9th.

The Rolt/Hamilton D Type Jaguar on its way to a worthy second place at Le Mans.

the Ferrari won from Hamilton and Rolt. A Cunningham driven by Spear/Johnston was 3rd and a privately entered C Type Jaguar driven by Laurent/Swaters was 4th. The D Type Jaguars of Moss/Walker and Whitehead/Wharton both retired. The DB3S Aston Martins had another unfortunate race, the Collins/Bira car retiring at 4 15 am and the Parnell/ Salvadori car expiring at 11 50 am. The fourth works DB3S in American colours and driven by Shelby/Frere retired just before midnight and a privately entered DB2/4 driven by Colas/de Silva Ramos retired at 6 am. A solitary Triumph TR2 driven by Wadsworth/ Brown finished the race in 15th position. The Lagonda had been running behind the Aston Martins and Thompson, after spinning the car in the rain after dark, had to withdraw from the race as the car's rear lights could not be repaired.

1955
The triumph and tragedy of the Silver Arrows

THE PROSPECTS FOR Formula 1 at the beginning of 1955 appeared to be excellent. The two new teams of Mercedes Benz and Lancia were already up and running and yet only the great Juan Fangio had managed to score more points than three Ferrari drivers in the 1954 World Championship. For 1955 the W196s came with variable wheelbases. Ferrari had produced the Tipo 555 Super Squalos with new space frames, even wider bodies, and more power, while the 250F Maserati remained a likely contender. The Connaughts, Coopers and Gordinis lacked power and sadly H.W.M. was gone, but the Vanwall's engine had been increased to a full 2.5 litres, and was being improved all the time. Tony Vandervell was a determined man and one who would not give up easily. There was also the prospect of a new 2.5 litre B.R.M. which would surely benefit from all the lessons that were learnt from the V16 cars.

Sadly, 1955 would be marred by tragedy. The death of eighty spectators at Le Mans when Pierre Levegh's Mercedes Benz 300SLR crashed into the crowd caused the French, German, Spanish, and Swiss Grands Prix to be cancelled, and motor racing would never again be allowed to take place in Switzerland. It might have resulted in motor racing being permanently banned more widely, but instead the sport was made progressively safer for both drivers and spectators in the years that followed through the efforts of Jackie Stewart, Louis Stanley and others.

During the winter of 1954/55 Stirling Moss signed a contract to drive for Mercedes Benz while Mike Hawthorn joined the Vanwall team. So Stirling, who had always wanted to drive British cars, would drive a German Mercedes while Mike exchanged his Italian Ferrari for a British Vanwall.

Eugenio Castellotti.

THE WORLD CHAMPIONSHIP SEASON
The Argentine Grand Prix. Buenos Aires: January 16

All four major teams were represented on the front row of the starting grid in Buenos Aires. Froilan Gonzales was fastest in practice with his Ferrari, Alberto Ascari second in the Lancia, Juan Fangio third in a Mercedes Benz and Jean Behra fourth in a Maserati. In the second row were Giuseppe Farina (Ferrari), Karl Kling (Mercedes Benz) and Harry Schell (Maserati) and in the third row Stirling Moss (Mercedes Benz), local boy Pablo Birger (Gordini), Hans Herrmann (Mercedes Benz) and Luigi Villoresi (Lancia). Eugenio

Castellotti was 12th fastest in the third Lancia, only 0.1 seconds slower than Villoresi. All the German cars were open wheeled models. Fangio led at the start of the race in extreme heat, from Ascari, Gonzales, Farina and Moss, but first Ascari got in front and then Gonzales, and it appeared that it could be anyone's race. However on the second lap there was a multiple crash which eliminated Behra, Kling, Carlos Menditeguy and Pablo Birger and, in addition Villoresi was forced to retire due to leaking fuel. While the battle continued at the front of the depleted field, Ascari ran over some oil on lap 22 and also crashed out of the race. The intense heat of Argentina was affecting all the drivers and Gonzales had to hand over his car to Farina who had previously been replaced in his car by Umberto Maglioli. Moss retired his car on lap 30 with fuel starvation and Fangio paused at his pit to be drenched with cold water! Fangio, who never ceased to amaze, then proceeded to recover the lead and to complete the race 1.5 minutes before the Ferrari, which had been shared by Gonzales/Farina/Trintignant, came in second. The Ferrari of Farina/Maglioli/Trintignant was third and a Mercedes Benz shared by Herrmann/Kling and Moss was fourth. Roberto Mieres drove his Maserati throughout and finished in fifth place five laps behind the winner. The Schell/Behra Maserati was sixth and the Luigi Musso/Schell Maserati seventh. It was altogether a most extraordinary race. Fangio's winning speed was 77.508mph and the fastest lap of the race, also by Fangio, was 80.809mph.

The Monaco Grand Prix. Monte Carlo: May 22

Only the times recorded on the first day of practice were allowed to count for the positions on the front row of the starting grid and only the first twenty cars were allowed to race. Juan Fangio and Stirling Moss were given specially designed cars with shorter wheelbases and out board brakes for the tight Monaco circuit and they were first and third in practice with Alberto Ascari's Lancia sandwiched between them at the front of the grid. Eugenio Castellotti (Lancia) and Jean Behra (Maserati) occupied the second row, and Roberto

Alberto Ascari in the D50 Lancia being closely followed by Eugenio Castellotti's car during the 1955 Monaco Grand Prix.

Signed photograph of Stirling Moss in his W196 Mercedes at Monaco.

Mieres (Maserati), Luigi Villoresi (Lancia) and Luigi Musso (Maserati) the third row. Andre Simon, who drove the third Mercedes Benz after Herrmann had crashed in practice, was 10th and Mike Hawthorn was 12th in the lone Vanwall. The local hero Louis Chiron was given a third Lancia and he was at the back of the starting grid with Jacques Pollet's Gordini. Fangio led narrowly at the start and at the end of the first lap the order was Fangio, Castellotti, Moss, and Ascari. Moss overtook Castellotti to catch up with Fangio and to run in formation well ahead the rest. Hawthorn's Vanwall retired with a broken throttle linkage. At about one third distance Castellotti hit a curb, slowed with a damaged rear tyre, and stopped at his pit for a new wheel. Next Fangio, who had been 40 seconds ahead of Ascari, stopped out on the circuit on lap 50 with transmission failure so that Moss now led from Ascari with Maurice Trintignant in third place. Moss once again appeared to have victory within his grasp but he was forced to stop with mechanical trouble on lap 81. He was able to claim ninth place at the end of the race merely by pushing the car over the line. The drama continued as Ascari, making a rare mistake as he came out of the tunnel, slid off the road and into the harbour. Thankfully, he quickly rose to the surface, leaving his car 15 ft below him, and was rescued. Sadly Alberto Ascari died four days later when testing a sports car at Monza. He had not entirely recovered from the injuries he had sustained at Monaco and a truly great driver was lost to the sport. He was wearing Castellotti's white helmet instead of his 'lucky' blue helmet which was being repaired. Like his father he was 36 years old when he died and both died in similar circumstances on the 26th day of the month. After all these events Trintignant became the surprised winner of the race, his Ferrari being followed by Castellotti's Lancia, and a Maserati which had been shared by Behra and Cesare Perdisa. Farina (Ferrari) was fourth, Villoresi (Lancia) fifth, Chiron

Castellotti's Lancia being followed by Moss and Fangio during the Monaco Grand Prix.

(Lancia) sixth, Pollet (Gordini) seventh, the Taruffi/Frere Ferrari eighth and Moss' Mercedes Benz ninth and last.

The race was won at 65.812mph and Fangio established the fastest lap at 68.704mph.

The Belgian Grand Prix. Spa: June 5

Following the tragic death of Alberto Ascari the Lancia team decided to withdraw from motor racing but Eugenio Castellotti was allowed to enter one car at Spa. He made the most of the opportunity by winning pole position on the starting grid. Juan Fangio and Stirling Moss shared the front row with him in their Mercedes ahead of Giuseppe Farina's Ferrari and Jean Behra's Maserati. Karl Kling was 6th fastest in the third Mercedes and Mike Hawthorn a lowly 9th in a Vanwall. Fangio and Moss cars had medium length chasses, Fangio's car had outboard front brakes and Moss' inboard, while Kling had a long chassis model. It would have been good to see the lone Lancia win but it was Fangio who led Castellotti at the start and Moss was soon past the Lancia too. Kling remained behind, followed by Farina's Tipo 555 Super Squalo Ferrari and Behra's 250F Maserati. After spinning and abandoning his car, Behra took over Roberto Mieres Maserati and set off again in ninth place. Hawthorn's Vanwall retired with gearbox trouble on lap 9, and on lap 17, to everyone's dismay, Castellotti's gearbox flew apart so the lone Lancia's race was over. With Fangio and Moss well ahead, Farina was now let into third place while Kling and Musso fought for the place behind him, but on lap 20 Luigi Musso pitted with a misfiring engine and Kling's race was ended on lap 22 because of a broken oil pipe. Fangio and Moss were able to ease off and Moss closed up on his team mate. Farina finished in third place, 1 minute 45 seconds behind Moss, followed by Paul Frere (Ferrari), Roberto Mieres/Jean Behra, Maurice Trintignant (Ferrari), Luigi Musso (Maserati), Cesare Perdisa (Maserati) and Louis Rosier (Maserati). Fangio's winning speed was 118.829mph and he drove the fastest lap of the race at 121.227mph.

Juan Fangio winning the Belgian Grand Prix in his W196 Mercedes Benz.

Juan Fangio closely followed by Stirling Moss in the 'W196 Train' during the Dutch Grand Prix.

The Dutch Grand Prix. Zandvoort: June 19

One week after the tragedy at Le Mans, the Mercedes Benz team turned up at Zandvoort with a variety of short and medium length W196 cars, all of which were tested by their drivers on Friday morning before the official practice began. After the practice on Friday and Saturday, Juan Fangio, driving a short 'Monaco' Mercedes, was in pole position, while Stirling Moss, with a medium length car, and Karl Kling in a second short model, occupied the remaining two places on the front row of the starting grid. Mike Hawthorn was immediately behind them in the new Tipo 555 Ferrari. Peter Walker drove Moss's 250F Maserati, Horace Gould his own car, while the three works Maseratis were driven by Jean Behra, Roberto Mieres and Luigi Musso. In the absence of Lancia Eugenio Castellotti drove a Tipo 555 Ferrari. At the start Fangio leapt into the lead but Musso's Maserati came through from the third row to capture second place. Moss was not to be separated from the Master for long and was soon past Musso to form 'the Train' by keeping close company with Fangio in front. Walker was immediately behind the works Italian cars until a cracked wheel caused him to spin out of contention. Kling, who had been running in fifth place behind his team mates and the Maseratis of Musso and Behra, spun on lap 24 and so his race too was ended. Gould spun his Maserati at the hairpin and, after laboriously getting it back on to the circuit and pointing in the right direction, retired at the completion of the lap. The two German cars were clearly dominant and, while Musso's Maserati was the best of the rest, the distance between him and Moss inexorably extended as the race wore on.

Fangio won with Moss only 0.3 secs behind him. Musso was third, a whole minute down, Mieres was fourth 1 lap behind. Castellotti and Behra were 3 laps down, Hawthorn was 5, Hernando da Silva Ramos (Gordini) and Louis Rosier (Maserati) 7, Jacques Pollet (Gordini) 8 and Johnnie Claes (Tipo 625 Ferrari) a full 12 laps in arrears. Fangio's average speed was 89.644mph but the fastest lap of the race was achieved by Mieres at 92.958mph.

The British Grand Prix. Aintree: July 16

For 1955 the British Grand Prix took place at Aintree near Liverpool and ever after Silverstone was challenged to raise its standards in order to gain the right to be chosen as venue for the race. Aintree was more like Silverstone than any of the Continental circuits and Stirling Moss was fastest throughout the practice sessions in a short wheelbase open wheeled W196 with outboard brakes. Juan Fangio was only 0.2 of a second slower in an identical car and Jean Behra completed the front row of the grid in his Maserati just one second behind the pole sitter. The two medium length Mercedes Benz of Karl Kling and Piero Taruffi also had outboard brakes and they made up the second row. Harry Schell's Vanwall was wedged between the Maseratis of Robert Mieres and Andre Simon immediately behind them. Mike Hawthorn was in 12th position, driving a Ferrari, Lance Macklin drove Stirling Moss' Maserati and Peter Collins the Owen Maserati. Kenneth McAlpine drove the fully streamlined Connaught and Jack Brabham made his Formula 1 debut in a rear engined 2.2 litre Bristol engined cooper with a sports car chassis.

Starting Grid

S. Moss	J.M. Fangio	J. Behra
Mercedes Benz	Mercedes Benz	Maserati
2 min 00.4 secs	2 min 00.6 secs	2 min 01.4 secs

K. Kling	P. Taruffi
Mercedes Benz	Mercedes Benz
2 min 02.0 secs	2 min 03.0 secs

R. Mieres	H. Schell	A. Simon
Maserati	Vanwall	Maserati
2 min 03.2 secs	2 min 03.8 secs	2 min 04.0 secs

L. Musso	E. Castellotti
Maserati	Ferrari
2 min 04.2 secs	2 min 05.0 secs

R. Manzon	J.M.Hawthorn	M. Trintignant
Gordini	Ferrari	Ferrari
2 min 05.0 secs	2 min 05.4 secs	2 secs 05.4 secs

A. Rolt	K. Wharton
Connaught	Vanwall
2 min 06.6 secs	2 min 08.4 secs

L. Macklin	K. McAlpine	H. Da Silva Ramos
Maserati	Connaught	Gordini
2 min 08.4 secs	2 min 09.6 secs	2 min 10.6 secs

L. Marr	R. Salvadori
Connaught	Maserati
2 min 11.6 secs	2 min 11.6 secs

J. Fairman	H. Gould	M. Sparken
Connaught	Maserati	Gordini
2 min 11.6 secs	2 min 11.8 secs	2 min 12.6 secs

P. Collins	J. Brabham
Maserati	Cooper-Bristol
2 min 13.4 secs	2 min 27.4 secs

Fangio's Mercedes Benz during the British Grand Prix at Aintree.

The two Mercedes leapt away as one at the start and Moss very narrowly led Fangio at Waterways. It was Fangio who was in front at the end of the first lap but Moss passed him again two laps later. Already the sceptics were beginning to question if this was to be a real race between the two drivers or merely a demonstration of the superiority of their cars. Behind the two, Behra was making it a contest with Kling and Taruffi, leading one to wonder to what extent the performance of the W196 was down to the sheer excellence of its leading drivers. Then Mieres passed Taruffi, adding fuel to the debate, and the British cars remained

Stirling Moss winning the 1955 British Grand Prix.

well down in the pack. Behra retired on lap 10 with a fractured oil pipe and the three Mercedes remained securely in front while Taruffi tried to shake off the Maseratis of Mieres and Musso.

Harry Schell was making up for having stalled his Vanwall at the start, climbing as high as eighth before being stopped when his accelerator pedal broke under extreme pressure on lap 21. Moss and Fangio remained in close company, occasionally exchanging the lead, and on lap 46 Hawthorn, suffering from the warm July afternoon, came in to hand his car to Castellotti. Schell took over Wharton's Vanwall now several laps down. As the race ran out Taruffi at last secured his fourth position so that the race presented a clean sweep for the Mercedes Benz team. Moss crossed the line just ahead of Fangio to become the first British driver to win the British Grand Prix. Afterwards Fangio declared that it had been a genuine race and that Moss was a worthy winner. For his part Stirling said that he floored the throttle coming out of the last bend in the race and had every intention of getting to the line first. Behind the Mercedes of Moss, Fangio, Kling and Taruffi came Musso, Hawthorn/Castellotti, Sparken, Macklin and the Wharton/Schell Vanwall 18 laps behind. Stirling Moss won the race at an average speed of 86.47mph and Fangio was just 0.2 seconds behind at the finish.

The fastest lap of the race was recorded by Moss at 89.70mph.

Result

1. S. Moss Mercedes Benz 3 hr. 7 min 21.2 secs
2. J.M. Fangio Mercedes Benz 3 hr. 7 min 21.4 secs
3. K. Kling Mercedes Benz 3 hr. 8 min 33.0 secs
4. P. Taruffi Mercedes Benz 1 lap behind
5. L. Musso Maserati
6. J.M. Hawthorn/E. Castellotti Ferrari 3 laps behind.
7. M. Sparken Gordini 9 laps behind
8. L. Macklin Maserati 11 laps behind
9. K. Wharton/H. Schell Vanwall 18 laps behind.

Retirements: R. Manzon Gordini transmission failure on lap 5, J. Behra Maserati fractured oil pipe on lap 19, A. Simon Maserati gearbox failure on lap 10, E. Castellotti Ferrari transmission failure on lap 17, L. Marr Connaught brake failure on lap 19, A. Rolt/P. Walker Connaught throttle failure on lap 20, H. Schell Vanwall snapped accelerator pedal on lap 21, H. Gould Maserati brake failure on lap 23, R. Salvadori Maserati gearbox failure on lap 24, H de Silva Ramos Gordini low oil pressure on lap 27, P. Collins Maserati clutch failure on lap 30, K. McAlpine Connaught fractured oil pipe on lap 31, J. Brabham Cooper-Bristol valve on lap 34, R. Mieres Maserati piston failure on lap 48, M. Trintignant Ferrari cracked cylinder head on lap 60.

The Italian Grand Prix. Monza: September 11

For 1955 the famous Monza circuit had been both lengthened and made much faster by the addition of two 180mph banked curves. The entire Lancia racing stable had been handed over to Enzo Ferrari who, in addition to his own team of Tipo 555 Super Squalo Ferraris, which were fitted with 5 speed gearboxes and driven by Mike Hawthorn, Umberto Maglioli and Maurice Trintignant, also fielded the unmodified Lancias for Eugenio Castellotti, Giuseppe Farina and Luigi Villoresi. The Lancias proved capable of offering Mercedes Benz serious opposition on the fast banked circuit but they threw their treads in practice and this led to them all being withdrawn from the race. Castellotti was given a Super Squalo Ferrari to drive instead and he was allowed to retain his fourth place on the grid. Mercedes Benz discovered that their 1954 long chassis car with a streamlined body was fastest and brought a second one over from Germany for the race. These, driven by Juan Fangio and Stirling Moss, were first and second in practice and Karl Kling was third in a long chassis open wheeled car with inboard brakes. Piero Taruffi drove a fourth W196, also with exposed wheels, which had a medium chassis and outboard brakes, and he was in the fourth row. Jean Behra had a streamlined Maserati with the tops of its wheels exposed. Peter Collins was on the fifth row of the grid with a works Maserati and Harry Schell and Ken Wharton were 11th and 14th in the Vanwalls.

It was Moss who led initially at the start from Fangio, Taruffi, Kling and Castellotti. Then, in the opening laps, Kling got past Taruffi and Fangio took the lead from Moss, the four silver cars settling down to draw away from all but Castellotti, who managed to hang on to them for a number of laps. Schell kept his Vanwall well placed in the middle of the Italian pack but then retired with a broken de Dion tube, all the cars having taken a battering on the banking. Musso caught up with Castellotti who had now dropped back from the fleeing W196s. However, on lap 19 Moss came in with a broken windshield caused by a stone flying up from Fangio's rear wheel. Typically, there was a spare one to hand at the pits and so he was soon off again although now in eighth place. Moss proceeded to break the lap record in an effort to catch up again with the leaders but his transmission broke so that he was out of the race on lap 28. Luigi Musso retired on lap 32 after being slowed with gearbox trouble and Kling stopped on the next lap with a broken gearbox. Fangio was able to slow down in the closing laps to enable Taruffi to make it a close finish. The two Mercedes crossed the line 45 seconds ahead of Castellotti who was followed at a distance by Behra in the streamlined Maserati. After Behra came Carlos Menditeguy (Maserati), Umberto Maglioli (Ferrari), Roberto Mieres (Maserati), Maurice Trintignant (Ferrari), and the American John Fitch driving a Maserati.

Fangio's winning speed was 128.494mph and Moss set the fastest lap of the race at 134.028mph.

After the race, and with Fangio having won the World Championship for the second year running, Mercedes Benz announced that it would withdraw from Formula 1. The W196 had won ten of its thirteen races. Mercedes Benz had also won the World Sports Car Championship with its team of 300SLRs but its racing department would remain closed until 2010.

The World Championship

Juan Fangio was the clear winner with 40 points. Moss had 23, Castellotti 12, Trintignant 11⅓, Farina 10⅓, and Taruffi 9. Kling came 10th with 5 points, Herrmann 22nd with 1 point.

The Non Championship Syracuse Grand Prix

Two B Type Connaughts were sent to Syracuse to be driven by Tony Brooks and Les Leston. The Maserati team was there in force with Luigi Musso and Luigi Villoresi at the wheels of their latest models but, to everyone's surprise, Brooks was quickest on Friday, the two British cars having arrived too late for the first day's practice. On Saturday the Italian drivers improved their times to take the first two places on the grid but Brooks was alongside them on the front row. Three Maseratis led at the end of the first lap of the race followed by the two Connaughts, but Brooks was in second place the following lap and pressed Musso for the lead. The two cars passed and re-passed each other until Brooks established a clear lead, setting a new lap record of 102.36mph on lap 55. Brooks won the race and so became the first British driver of a British car to win a Grand Prix since Seagrave won the San Sebastian Grand Prix in a Sunbeam in 1924. The Connaught was minutely examined by the surprised officials after the race to make sure that it conformed in every respect to the regulations!

Tony Brooks' Connaught at the start of the Syracuse Grand Prix with the 250F Maseratis of Musso (12) and Villoresi (24).

Harry Schell driving the 2.5 litre Vanwall at Castle Combe in 1955.

Monte Carlo Rally

The 96 Glasgow starters had to encounter hazardous conditions in which snow ploughs were only partially successful in clearing a path for them. The first of the cars to start from Glasgow was a Ford Zephyr and it was followed by an Austin A35. Another Zephyr, driven by the racing driver Cuth Harrison was the first to arrive at Dover to board the *Lord Warden* early the following morning. Only 48 of the 319 entrants retired and these because of the kind of irritating mechanical failures that should not have occurred. It underlined the value of the Monte in improving the reliability of cars for the ordinary motorist.

The overall winner was a privately entered Sunbeam Talbot Mark III which started from Oslo, driven by Per Malling and Gunnar Fadum. The pair emerged as clear winners following the 180 mile high speed section, the acceleration, reversing and braking test, and the race over the Monaco circuit. A tiny Dyna Panhard driven by G. Gilard and R. Dugat was second and the more substantial Mercedes Benz 220 of H. Gerdum and Dr J. Kubling was third. Gatsonides and Becquarts finished in seventh place in an Aston Martin DB2/4. The Coupe des Dames was won by Sheila Van Dam and the Concours de Confort again by W.M. Couper with P. Fillingham in a Armstrong-Siddeley Sapphire.

Mille Miglia

Mercedes Benz returned to the Mille Miglia in 1955 to prepare for the race with even greater thoroughness than before. They established their headquarters at Gardone long before the event with their drivers, Fangio, Kling, Moss and Herrmann. Kling covered nearly 30,000 miles in practice while Fangio joined them too late to put in nearly as much practice as the others. Lancia was an absentee, concentrating on its promising Formula 1 programme. Ferrari brought cars for Taruffi, Castellotti, Maglioli and Paolo Marzotto. Stirling Moss had

Stirling Moss and Denis Jenkinson in their 300SLR Mercedes Benz immediately before the start of the 1955 Mille Miglia.

Stirling Moss on his way to winning the Mille Miglia.

Denis Jenkinson as his navigator, in place of co-driver John Fitch, and Jenkinson's pace notes were to contribute to his success. Hans Herrmann was accompanied by his mechanic Herman Eger. David Brown had hoped to enter two V12 Lagondas but insufficient power could be extracted from their engines. Instead Frere and Wisdom were given DB2/4s to compete in the G.T. category against the Mercedes 300SLs while Collins had a DB3S. In the race the DB3S was to suffer a thrown tread followed by a seized engine.

The first of the smaller cars set off at 9 p.m. on the Saturday but it was not until the next morning that the Mercedes team was released from the starting ramp, Fangio at 6 58, Kling at 7 01, Herrmann at 7 04 and Moss at 7 22, their racing numbers as usual indicating their start times. The Ferraris of Castellotti and Taruffi left at 7 23 and 7 27.

Castellotti overtook Moss at Padova, the two racing at tremendous speed. Marzotto's car threw a tread and could not continue as his spare tyre turned out to be the wrong size! Moss passed Castellotti at the Ravena check point and was leading the race as he reached Rome. Taruffi was then lying in second place with Herrmann third, Kling fourth and Fangio fifth. After this Kling crashed, Taruffi was forced to retire with a broken transmission, and Moss went on to win at the record speed of 93.53mph in 10 hrs, 7 mins and 48 secs. Fangio was second, coming in on seven cylinders, and Maglioli third. It was Stirling's third Mille Miglia and one that he had been determined to win. In *All My Races* Stirling Moss describes how at one point his car took off from the brow of a hill, twice hit some straw bales, and spun when his brakes grabbed. The Mille Miglia was never an event for the faint hearted! His win was perhaps the greatest achievement of his illustrious career and it was only the second time that the event was won by a non Italian.

Le Mans

Le Mans was expected to be a close and exciting contest between the D Type Jaguars and the 300SLR Mercedes Benz in their latest forms. The Mercedes were equipped with large air brakes which rose up behind their drivers to slow the cars down as they approached

Juan Fangio leading Mike Hawthorn and Eugenio Castellotti before the tragic accident during the 1955 Le Mans 24 Hour race.

The Aston Martin DB3S of Roy Salvadori leading Peter Collins' identical car through the Esses at Le Mans.

corners to compensate for the fact that, unlike the long nosed Jaguars, they had drum brakes. Jaguar had three cars to be driven by Hawthorn/Bueb, Rolt/Hamilton and Beauman/ Dewis, and the 300SLRs were driven by Fangio/Moss, Fitch/Levegh and Kling/Simon. The drivers for the 4.4 litre Ferraris were Maglioli/Hill, Castellotti/Marzotto and Trintignant/Schell. The 4.5 litre V12 Lagonda was assigned to Parnell/Poore and the 2.9 litre Aston Martin DB3Ss to Collins/Frere, Salvadori/Walker and Riseley Pritchard/ Brooks. Macklin and Leston drove an Austin Healey 100S. The team of Bristol 450s now had open 2 seater bodies.

At the start the two Ferraris of Castellotti and Maglioli led the Jaguars of Hawthorn and Beauman while Parnell was in 9th place in the Lagonda. Then, as the race began to settle down the order was Castellotti, Hawthorn and Fangio. At around 4 30 p.m. Fangio got past Hawthorn and a fierce dual began which was reminiscent of their epic race at Rheims in 1953. Castellotti retired with a blown engine and the Jaguar and Mercedes charged round lap after lap only feet apart. The 24 hour race had developed into a Grand Prix and it surely couldn't last. Then at 6 30 p.m. the unthinkable happened. Hawthorn had just lapped Levegh and, with Fangio hot on his heels, was anxious not to lose a faction of a second in coming into his pit. He overtook Macklin's Austin Healey on the narrow pit straight and swerved sharply across it in order to duck into the Jaguar pit where Bueb was waiting to take over. Macklin was forced to swerve to avoid the Jaguar and Levegh had to take avoiding action in attempting to miss the Austin Healey. Before the fatal contact was made Levegh raised his hand to warn Fangio who was just behind him and who later said the gesture saved his life. Levegh's 300SLR hit the back of the Austin Healey at speed, bounced off the opposite bank, splitting in two as it burst into flames, and scythed into the packed crowd of spectators. Poor Levegh was thrown out and instantly killed and eighty spectators were also killed in what looked like a battle field, many of them being decapitated by the flying engine. Fangio, reacting to Levegh's warning, managed to squeeze through unharmed and continued to lead from Hawthorn while everyone tried to take stock of the situation. It was decided to let the race run for the full 24 hours to avoid both the pit area being obstructed by crowds of spectators and the surrounding roads becoming blocked to emergency vehicles. Orders came from Stuttgart for the Mercedes Benz team to withdraw and to return immediately to Germany which it did before the end of the race. The Hawthorn/Bueb Jaguar won a hollow victory from the Aston Martin of Collins/Frere.

Many blamed Mike Hawthorn for the accident but others dispute this and, had the consequences been less tragic, it would merely have been described as a racing accident. A major cause was the narrowness of the pits straight and this was rectified for 1956. It was without doubt the worst disaster ever to have occurred in the history of motor racing.

The Swaters/Claes Jaguar was 3rd and a 1.5 litre Porsche driven by Frankenberg/ Polensky was fourth overall in addition to winning the Index of Performance. The Lagonda retired when its fuel escaped after its tank hadn't been properly secured. Of the other two works Jaguars, that driven by Rolt/Hamilton retired in the fifth hour and the one driven by Beaman/Dewis retired in the eleventh hour. A D Type Jaguar entered by Briggs Cunningham and driven by Walters/Spear retired after seven hours. The Aston Martins of Brooks/Riseley Pritchard retired in the ninth hour and that of Salvadori/Walker in the tenth hour. Of the drivers of three works M.G.A.s Miles/Lockett finished in 12th place and Lund/Waeffler 17th, while the car driven by Jacobs/Flynn retired after crashing in the sixth hour. Works Triumph TR2s finished 14th, driven by Dickson/Sanderson, 15th driven by Hadley/Richardson and 19th driven by Brooke/Morris-Goodall. A lone works Lotus driven by Chapman/Flockhart was disqualified during the 12th hour after being in 27th place.

The Peter Walker/Dennis Poore Aston Martin DB3S which won the Goodwood Nine Hours Race in 1955.

Targa Florio

Peter Collins had impressed Mercedes Benz with his performance with a works Aston Martin DB3S in the 1955 Tourist Trophy Race in Dundrod and so he was invited to share with Stirling Moss a 300SLR in the Targa Florio, the oldest road race for sports cars in the world. Moss set a cracking pace from the start and led until his car slid off the road on some loose stones, coming to rest 12 feet below the road. With the help of spectators the car was returned to the road but 12 minutes had been lost when Collins took over the controls of the battered vehicle. Collins also dented the bodywork when he banged it against a wall but by the 8th lap he had regained the lead and was 11 seconds ahead of the Eugenio Castellotti/Robert Manzon Ferrari in second place. Ferrari mistakenly brought Robert Manzon in after he had only driven 2 laps which meant that he would have to do another short stint, inevitably losing time with the changeover. Moss took over the 300SLR for the last 5 of the 13 laps of the race to win, 4 minutes 42 seconds ahead of the Fangio/Kling Mercedes with the Castellotti/Manzon Ferrari in third place. As a result of this and the previous events the Mercedes Benz team won the World Sports Car Championship for 1955.

1956
The emergence of the Lancia-Ferrari

WITH THE ABSENCE of the Mercedes Benz team in 1956 it remained to be seen which would be the best of the remaining teams. The Lancia-Ferraris which appeared in the entry lists were only slightly modified Lancia D50s at the beginning of the Season but they were increasing modified as time went on and it has been suggested that their handling qualities deteriorated rather than improved as a result! The pannier tanks of the Lancia-Ferraris became merely used to house their exhaust pipes, all the fuel being carried in their tails instead. Maserati had the constantly improving 250F at its disposal plus the services of Stirling Moss. Juan Fangio decided to postpone his retirement after the fall of President Peron and chose to drive a Lancia-Ferrari with Eugenio Castellotti, Luigi Musso and Peter Collins. In Argentina Ferrari also had amongst its weaponry an experimental Super Squalo with a Lancia engine and a Lancia with a Ferrari engine. Tony Vandervell was getting serious, now fielding entirely new cars with space frames designed by Colin Chapman and tear drop bodies by Frank Costin. B.R.M. had introduced its 2.5 litre 4 cylinder P25 at Oulton Park at the end of 1955 where Peter Collins had demonstrated its remarkable turn of speed. It was a beautiful little car and, as with the original P15 B.R.M., looked its best in its earliest form. Mike Hawthorn and Tony Brooks both signed up to drive the new cars in 1956. A new and interesting Bugatti appeared at Rheims, designed by Columbo and featuring a transversely placed straight eight engine. Sadly there were not the resources to develop the car and so it was not seen again. In the 1960s the Bugatti factory would be used to build air frames for the Concorde.

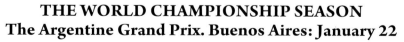

Luigi Musso.

THE WORLD CHAMPIONSHIP SEASON
The Argentine Grand Prix. Buenos Aires: January 22

Neither the Vanwalls or the B.R.M.s were at Buenos Aires for the Argentine Grand Prix but Mike Hawthorn was there to drive the Owen Maserati. The Lancia-Ferraris were fastest in practice in the order of Juan Fangio, whose practice sessions were interrupted by mechanical problems, Eugenio Castellotti and Luigi Musso. The three were joined on the front row of the grid by Jean Behra's Maserati. The second row contained the Maseratis of Froilan Gonzales, Carlo Menditeguy and Stirling Moss while behind them were Mike Hawthorn, Peter Collins (Ferrari) Olivier Gendebien (Lancia-Ferrari) and Francisco Landi (Maserati).

Musso led the race initially but was soon overtaken by Gonzales on his home ground. He in turn was caught by local boy Menditeguy who was followed by Moss, Castellotti and Gonzales, with Musso relegated to fifth place. Fangio came into his pit with problems with his fuel pump and finally retired on lap 23, immediately afterwards taking over Musso's car. Gonzales retired on lap 25 with mechanical trouble and, when approaching half distance, Castellotti's race ended with a broken gearbox. Menditeguy retired with a broken half shaft and Moss was in trouble with a misfiring engine so that Fangio went past to lead the race. Behra quickly followed him to run in second place and Moss retired with a sick engine on lap 82. So Fangio won from Behra at a speed of 79.386mph. Hawthorn must have been pleased with his third place in a privately entered Maserati and he was followed by Landi/ Gerino Gerini (Maserati), Gendebien (Lancia-Ferrari) and Alberto Uria/Gonzales (Maserati). The fastest lap of the race was recorded by Fangio at 83.105mph.

Monaco Grand Prix. Monte Carlo: May 11

When Stirling Moss received my painting of him winning the Monaco Grand Prix in 1956 in a 250F Maserati he wrote: 'A great car in a great race'. Two of the new B.R.M.s arrived at Monaco for Mike Hawthorn and Tony Brooks but they encountered valve problems during practice and were withdrawn from the race. Hawthorn's time would have put him 10th on the grid and Brook's 12th. The two entirely new Vanwalls, driven by Harry Schell and Maurice Trintignant were 5th and 6th. and so it seemed that Great Britain had at least one competitive team at last. Yet the Lancia-Ferraris of Juan Fangio and Eugenio Castellotti were on either side of the Maserati of Stirling Moss at the front of the grid, and the grid positions at Monaco were, as ever, all important. Peter Collins was back in 9th place with his Lancia-Ferrari. On a beautiful May afternoon it was Moss who made the best start and

Stirling Moss winning the Monaco Grand Prix in 1956 in his works 250F Maserati.

B. G. Apps '87.

he led Castellotti, Fangio and Schell around the opening lap. Then on the second lap Fangio spun, causing several rapidly approaching cars to take sudden avoiding action. Both Musso and Schell left the road and their cars were too damaged to continue. Fangio got going again behind Moss, Castellotti, Collins and Behra and he overtook Castellotti when the clutch on the Italian's Lancia-Ferrari began to fail. The Argentinian moved up to second place behind Moss by lap 25 but seven laps later he uncharacteristically hit the harbour wall bending his rear wheel. Castellotti took his place in the stricken car when he arrived at the pits. At 50 laps Moss led Collins by half a minute and behind them were Behra, Castellotti and Manzon. Then Fangio took over Collins' car, dropping it down to third place and he was 47 seconds behind Moss when he recovered second place from Behra on lap 70. Further drama occurred when Cesare Perdisa's brakes locked just as Moss was to lap him and when the two cars touched the bonnet of the leading Maserati was loosened. Fangio, in gaining on Moss, set the fastest lap of the race at 67.388mph while driving on the limit, and he was only 6.1 seconds behind the Maserati at the end. Moss won at a speed of 64.942mph and after the Collins/Fangio Lancia-Ferrari came Behra's Maserati, the Fangio/Castellotti Lancia-Ferrari, de Silva Ramos (Gordini), Bayol/Pilette (Gordini), Perdisa (Maserati) and Gould (Maserati). Schell retired after crashing on the second lap and Trintignant retired on lap 11 due to his engine overheating. Fangio recorded the fastest lap of the race on lap 100.

The Belgian Grand Prix. Spa: June 3

The B.R.M.s failed to arrive at Spa because the team's efforts were concentrated on trying to overcome the mechanical problems which had come to light at Monaco. Hence Hawthorn was available but as both Ferrari and Maserati wanted his services and an argument ensued between the two teams he declined to race for either of them. Stirling Moss found himself once more surrounded by Lancia-Ferraris on the starting grid, Juan Fangio once again securing pole with, on this occasion, Peter Collins in third place. Behind these three were Jean Behra's Maserati and Eugenio Castellotti's Lancia-Ferrari. Then came the Vanwalls of Harry Schell and Maurice Trintignant, and Paul Frere in the third Lancia-Ferrari. Luigi Villoresi's Maserati was 11th. Paul Scotti's Connaught 12th and Andre Pilette's Lancia-Ferrari 15th and last alongside Horace Gould's privately entered Maserati.

Juan Fangio's Lancia-Ferrari during the 1956 Belgian Grand Prix.

Stirling Moss in the 250F
Maserati during the Belgian
Grand Prix.

Moss made an excellent start and was followed by Castellotti, Collins Behra and Fangio. The last named soon began to make amends for his tardy start and went into the lead on lap 5. The order was then Fangio, Moss, Collins, Castellotti but on lap 11 Moss lost one of his rear wheels and he managed to park his car safely on the grass. Returning to the pits on foot Moss took over Cesare Perdisa's car and resumed the race in sixth place behind Schell's Vanwall, Castellotti having already retired with transmission trouble. On lap 24 Fangio's race was also ended when his transmission failed, leaving Collins out in front with a clear lead. Paul Frere's Lancia-Ferrari passed a slowing Behra into second place and Moss, establishing the fastest lap of the race at 124.010mph, passed Behra too. So Collins won his first World Championship Grand Prix by 1 minute 48.6 seconds at a speed of 118.442mph from his Belgian team mate. The Perdisa/Moss Maserati was third, Schell (Vanwall) fourth, Villoresi (Maserati) fifth, Pilette (Lancia-Ferrari) sixth, Behra (Maserati) seventh and Rosier (Maserati) eighth, and last of them being three laps being behind the winner.

French Grand Prix. Rheims: July 7

In the continued absence of the B.R.M.s Mike Hawthorn was released to drive a Vanwall in the French Grand Prix at Rheims and he won 100 bottles of champagne for being the first driver to achieve a 200 kph lap! Colin Chapman was to have driven a third Vanwall but he collided with Hawthorn during practice when his brakes failed and, as a result, Vanwall were left with only two complete cars for the race. The front row of the grid was wholly occupied by the Lancia-Ferraris of Juan Fangio, Eugenio Castellotti and Peter Collins. Harry Schell was alone in his Vanwall on the second row and behind him were Hawthorn and the Maseratis of Jean Behra and Stirling Moss. Then came Alfonso de Portago (Lancia-Ferrari) and Luigi Villoresi (Maserati) and in 18th place Maurice Trintignant in the new Bugatti. Villoresi's car stalled at the start but everyone avoided him, and the order at the front was Castellotti, Fangio, Collins, Schell, and Moss in the first of the Maseratis. Schell

Fangio's Lancia-Ferrari at Rheims during the 1956 French Grand Prix.

and Moss dropped back with assorted problems and it was Hawthorn who was next up to the three Lancia-Ferraris. Schell retired on lap 6 with engine trouble and Hawthorn handed over to him four laps later as he was tired from his recent 12 hour race at Rheims with a Jaguar. Maurice Trintignant was ahead of the French Gordinis but well back, and Schell resumed the race in eighth place. Moss retired on lap 11 with a broken gear lever, but Schell was actually lapping faster in the Vanwall than Fangio's Lancia-Ferrari at the front! Passing Jean Behra and Olivier Gendebien (Lancia-Ferrari), Schell moved up to fourth place as, further down the field, the Bugatti retired with an inoperable throttle. On lap 31 Schell had passed the Lancia-Ferraris of Collins and Castellotti and had only Fangio ahead of him. Fangio responded to this threat by widening the gap, and the other two Lancia-Ferrari relegated the Vanwall to fourth place again. Running as a team the Lancia-Ferraris raced down the straights side by side giving the Vanwall no room to get by them! Eventually Schell slowed and stopped to have his injection pump replaced. Out of the running, he had nevertheless given fair warning of the new Vanwall's potential. Fangio was the next to stop with a leaking fuel pipe and couldn't improve on fourth place after returning to the fray. So

Maurice Trintignant with the Bugatti 251 during the French Grand Prix.

Collins won two races in succession 0.3 seconds ahead of Castellotti. Behra was third in his Maserati, Fangio fourth, Perdisa/Moss fifth, Rosier (Maserati) sixth, Francisco Godia (Maserati) seventh, de Silva Ramos (Gordini) eighth, Manzon (Gordini) ninth, Hawthorn/Schell tenth, and Pilette (Gordini) eleventh and last. Peter Collins' average speed for the race was 122.287mph and Fangio's consolation was the fastest lap of the race at 127.369mph.

The British Grand Prix, Silverstone: July 14

The B.R.M.s came to Silverstone with every hope of impressing the crowd and silencing their sceptics. Three cars were entered for Mike Hawthorn, Tony Brooks and Ron Flockhart, and Hawthorn was on the front row of the starting grid with Stirling Moss Maserati) and Juan Fangio (Lancia-Ferrari) to his right and Peter Collins (Lancia-Ferrari) to his left. Brooks was on the third row in the second B.R.M. and Flockhart back in the sixth row. Froilan Gonzales drove the leading Vanwall and this promised to add considerable interest to the race. Archie Scott Brown drove a Connaught, and Bob Gerard his faithful but outclassed Cooper-Bristol.

The Starting Grid

P.Collins	J.M.Hawthorn	J.M Fangio	S Moss
Lancia-Ferrari	B.R.M	Lancia-Ferrari	Maserati
1 min 43 secs	1 min 43 secs	1 min 42 secs	1 min 41 secs

	R. Salvadori	J.F.Gonzales	H.Schell
	Maserati	Vanwall	Vanwall
	1 min 44 secs	1 min 44 secs	1 min 44 secs

D. Titterington	A. Scott Brown	C.A.S.Brooks	E.Castellotti
Connaught	Connaught	B.R.M	Lancia-Ferrari
1 min 46 secs	1 min 45 secs	1 min 45 secs	1 min 44 secs

	H. Gould	J.Behra	A de Portago
	Maserati	Maserati	Lancia-Ferrari
	1 min 48 secs	1 min 47 secs	1 min 47 secs

R. Manzon	R. Flockhart	M. Trintignant	C. Perdisa
Gordini	B.R.M	Vanwall	Maserati
1 min 49 secs	1 min 49 secs	1 min 49 secs	1 min 49 secs

	J.Fairman	B.Halford	L.Villoresi
	Connaught	Maserati	Maserati
	1 min 51 secs	1 min 51 secs	1 min 50 secs

F.Godia	U.Maglioli	P.Emery	F.R.Gerard
Maserati	Maserati	Emeryson	Cooper-Bristol
1 min 55 secs	1 min 54 secs	1 min 54 secs	1 min 53 secs

	J,Brabham	L.Rosier	H.de Silva Ramos
	Maserati	Maserati	Gordini
	2 min 01 secs	1 min 59 secs	1 min 56 secs

B.G Apps

Stirling Moss driving a works
250F Maserati leading the1956
British Grand Prix.

At the fall of the flag the B.R.M.s of Hawthorn and Brooks out-accelerated all the other cars, Hawthorn shooting into an early lead. Disappointingly, Gonzales immediately stopped with a broken drive shaft while Brooks magnificently came up from the third row to take second place in front of Juan Fangio, Harry Schell, and Eugenio Castellotti, while Stirling Moss was back in ninth place. Flockhart's B.R.M. pulled out on lap 2 with engine trouble. Fangio managed to get past Brooks on the seventh lap but Brooks retrieved his position when Fangio, after spinning at Becketts, had to restart behind Schell, Castellotti,

Juan Fangio in his Lancia-
Ferrari winning the British
Grand Prix on July 14.

Roy Salvadori, driving a privately entered Maserati, and Collins. Next Moss, having made rapid progress through the field, passed Brooks on lap 11 and, after closing on Hawthorn, took the lead. Then the B.R.M. gremlins reasserted themselves on lap 24 when Hawthorn was forced to retire with a leaking oil seal and on lap 40 Brooks stopped with a broken throttle. Soon after Brooks returned to the race his B.R.M. spun and he was thrown out as his car overturned and caught fire. Fortunately he was not seriously hurt but he was taken to hospital with facial injuries. The B.R.M.s had proved to be exceptionally fast but unreliable, not to say dangerous! Fangio passed Salvadori to lead the race followed by Collins while Moss stopped to take on oil. On lap 59 Collins came into his pit with low oil pressure and he took over Alfonso de Portago's Lancia-Ferrari. Moss stopped again for adjustments and eventually retired on lap 59 with a broken rear axle. So Fangio emerged as the winner at a speed of 98.65mph. The fastest lap of the race was recorded by Moss at 102.10mph.

Results
1. J. Fangio Lancia-Ferrari 2 hr. 59 min 47 secs.
2. A. De Portago/P. Collins Lancia-Ferrari 1 lap behind.
3. J. Behra Maserati 2 laps behind.
4. J. Fairman Connaught 3 laps behind.
5. H. Gould Maserati 4 laps behind.
6. L. Villoresi Maserati 5 laps behind.
7. C. Perdisa Maserati 6 laps behind.
8. F. Godia Maserati 7 laps behind.
9. R. Manzon Gordini .
10. E. Castellotti/A de Portago Lancia-Ferrari 9 laps behind.
11. F. R. Gerard Cooper-Bristol 13 laps behind.

Retirements: J.F. Gonzales Vanwall driveshaft on lap 1, R. Flockhart B.R.M. engine on lap 2, J. Brabham Maserati engine on lap 4, P. Emery Emeryson ignition on lap 12, A. Scott Brown Connaught axle on lap17, U. Maglioli Maserati gearbox on lap 22, B. Halford Maserati piston on lap 23, J.M. Hawthorn B.R.M. oil seal on lap 24, L. Rosier Maserati magneto on lap 24, C.A.S. Brooks B.R.M. crash on lap 41, R. Salvadori Maserati fuel feed on lap 59, P. Collins Lancia-Ferrari oil pressure on lap 64, M. Trintignant Vanwall fuel feed on lap 70, H de Silva Ramos Gordini axle on lap 72, D. Titterington Connaught engine on lap 75, H. Schell Vanwall fuel feed on lap 87, S. Moss Maserati axle on lap 94.

The German Grand Prix. Nurburgring: August 5

There were no B.R.M.s or Vanwalls at the Nurburgring and only two Gordinis to challenge the might of the Italian cars. On the front row of the grid were the Lancia-Ferraris of Juan Fangio, Peter Collins and Eugenio Castellotti and the Maserati of Stirling Moss. Roy Salvadori was in 8th spot in a Centro Sud 250F Maserati. At the start Collins took an immediate lead but was soon overtaken by Fangio. The two were followed by Moss and Castellotti while Fangio broke the lap record which had been established by Hermann Lang's 3 litre supercharged Mercedes W154 way back in 1939. Luigi Piotti (Maserati). Giorgio Scarlatti (Ferrari) and Robert Manzon (Gordini) were all early retirements. Fangio and Collins drew well away from Moss who in turn led Jean Behra (Maserati), Salvadori (Maserati), Alfonso de Portago (Lancia-Ferrari), Umberto Maglioli (Maserati), Luigi Musso (Lancia-Ferrari) and Harry Schell, now driving a Maserati. It was reminiscent of the previous year when Fangio, then driving a W196 Mercedes Benz, had another young English driver on his tail. This ended when Collins pitted on lap 9 just before losing consciousness through the fumes from a fuel leak. Castellotti took over Musso's car after his had stopped with a faulty magneto, only to spin and stall his engine. Collins was back in the race driving de Portago's car but spun and retired on lap 15 having recovered to third place. The race was won by Fangio at 85.535mph and he was followed across the line by Moss and Behra, Moss being only 18 seconds behind the winner. Only five finished, Francisco Godia and Louis Rosier being fourth and fifth in their Maseratis. The fastest lap of the race was recorded by Fangio at 87.731mph.

The Italian Grand Prix. Monza: September 2

Three Vanwalls were at Monza for Piero Taruffi, Harry Schell and Maurice Trintignant, but it was the might of the Lancia-Ferraris which dominated the front row with Juan Fangio, Eugenio Castellotti and Luigi Musso. Taruffi was fourth in the leading Vanwall with the Maseratis of Jean Behra and Stirling Moss alongside him on the second row. Peter Collins was back in 7th. place and the Vanwalls of Harry Schell and Maurice Trintignant 10th and 11th. Jack Fairman's Connaught was 15th. Les Leston's and Ron Flockhart's Connaughts were 19th and 23rd on the now familiar grid of eight rows of three cars.

In the opening laps Musso and Castellotti fought for the lead with such exuberance that both had to stop for new tyres after only five laps. Fangio, Moss, Collins and Schell followed them at a sensible distance and inherited the front of the field when they stopped. Alfonso de Portago, driving one of the Lancia-Ferraris, lost a tread at 160mph and managed to slide all the way down the banking at reducing speed to drive back to his pit. Castellotti, driving on the limit again, suffered the same fate and crashed out of the race. Collins stopped for tyres on lap 11 and Fangio, Moss and Schell continued to take turns to lead, this being the first time that a Vanwall had led a World Championship Grand Prix. Behra was in fourth place ahead of Musso, Maglioli and Collins, and Fangio came in on lap 19 when the steering arm of his car failed. Out in front Moss drew away from Schell, and Musso ran in second place when the Vanwall driver came in for fuel on lap 28 after having started with a tank that was half empty. Four laps later Schell was out of the race with transmission trouble. Collins was now in third place behind Moss and Musso, but when Collins came in for a further tyre check he generously handed his car over to Fangio - even though it probably cost him the World Championship. It was now Moss's race but he ran out of fuel out on the circuit with only five laps to go. Fortunately his team mate Luigi Piotti, down in seventh place, came along and pushed his car back to the pits with the nose cowl of his own Maserati. Since it was the car rather than a mere mortal that did the pushing it was not officially deemed to be outside assistance and, in the course of breaking the lap record, Moss went on to win the race, Musso having stopped on lap 47 also with a broken steering arm. Behind Moss' Maserati the Collins/ Fangio Lancia-Ferrari came second and Flockhart's Connaught a very creditable third. Then came Luigi Piotti (Maserati), Toulo de Graffenried (Maserati), Fangio/ Castellotti (Lancia-Ferrari), Andre Simon (Gordini), and Roy Salvadori (Maserati). The winning speed was 129.734mph and the fastest lap was also recorded by Moss at 135.407mph.

The World Championship

Juan Fangio won the World Championship with 30 points, Stirling Moss was second with 27 and Peter Collins third with 25. Jack Fairman came 10th with his Connaught and Mike Hawthorn 12th with the 4 points he had gained in Argentina.

Monte Carlo Rally

Fog was the greatest hazard faced by the competitors in the Monte Carlo Rally in 1956 and in Monte Carlo the 150 mile mountain test eliminated a number of the ninety cars which had previously come through unscathed. The mountain test replaced the race on the Grand

Archie Scott Brown in the B Type Connaught during the Richmond Trophy Race at Goodwood on April 2nd.

Mike Hawthorn leading the *Daily Express* International Trophy Race at Silverstone on May 5.

Duncan Hamilton's 3.4 litre Jaguar and Paul Frere's Mark VII at Silverstone during the International Trophy Race meeting at Silverstone.

Signed painting of Tony Brooks driving the P25 B.R.M. in its original form during the Aintree 200 Miles Race in 1956.

Prix circuit and *Motor Sport* approvingly described it as a "free-for-all 'Targa Florio.'" In all 21 Fords entered the Rally and the works cars were equipped with reclining seats and hoods to place over their headlamps in foggy conditions. 233 cars reached Monte Carlo having completed the 2,600 mile road section, and the outright winners were Ronnie Adams, Frank Bigger and Derek Johnston in a Mark VII Jaguar. A Mercedes 220 came second and a D.K.W. third. Equal third were P. Harper and D Humphrey in their Sunbeam and M. Grosgogeant and P. Biagini in a D.K.W. J. Ray and J. Cutts came 10th in another Sunbeam and, with the additional help of Miss Van Damm, the Mark III Sunbeam Talbots won the Team Prize. Mike Couper and Pat Fillingham won the Coupe de Confort with an Austin A90.

The Mille Miglia

Stirling Moss drove a works 3.5 litre Maserati with Denis Jenkinson in 1956. Fangio and Castellotti had V12 290 Mille Miglia Ferraris, Collins and Musso 4 cylinder 860 Monzas and Gendebien a 250 GT. Moss started from the ramp at 5 54am, preceded by the Ferraris of Castellotti, Collins and Taruffi. Heavy rain persisted and Jenkinson recorded that it penetrated the car from underneath as well as from above so that they were fighting the elements as they competed against other cars. Moss was passed by Musso when travelling at 130mph and then overtook him in turn as he approached a bend at high speed. He and 'Jenks' overtook John Heath who sadly was killed when he crashed later in the race. At Pescara they were told that they were lying sixth overall and fourth in their class. Castellotti was leading and von Trips was in second place in his 300SL Mercedes. Stirling's race ended abruptly when all four wheels locked up at 70mph. His Maserati crashed into a stone wall, bounced back across the road, through a barbed wire fence and up a bank before crashing back to come to an abrupt end, fortunately neither Moss nor Jenkinson being seriously injured. Moss recorded that a barbed wire fence damaged his helmet, windscreen and watch

The 860 Monza Ferrari of Peter Collins and Louis Klemantaski speeding through heavy rain during the 1956 Mille Miglia.

but he escaped with a minor scratch on his face. In the meantime Collins was lying in second place at Rome, 14 minutes behind the flying Castellotti, and he closed the gap to 10 minutes before an oil leak obscured his vision. Having to complete the race without a visor, he still managed to finish second behind Castellotti. Musso was third, and Fangio fourth.

Le Mans

Following the tragic accident of the previous year the Le Mans pit straight was widened and re designed to avoid a similar incident happening again. The rules were also revised to limit prototypes, as opposed to standard production cars, to 2.5 litres. The capacity of fuel tanks was restricted to 29 gallons and re fuelling was not allowed in less than 34 laps. A full width wind shield was made compulsory and a flexible tonneau cover.

Three 2.5 litre Testa Rosa Ferraris were entered for Hill/Simon, de Portago/Hamilton and Trintignant/Gendebien. A DBR/250 Aston Martin, smaller and lighter than the DB3S, was provided for Parnell/Brooks, DB3S models being driven by Moss/Collins and Walker/Salvadori. There were also 2.5 litre Gordinis and Talbots.

The works Jaguars were clearly the fastest cars in the race and it was Hawthorn who led from the start. Then the Frere/Titteringon and Fairman/Wharton Jaguars were eliminated when Fairman, Frere and de Portago all collided on the first lap. The Hawthorn/Bueb Jaguar car came into the pits with fuel injection trouble and lost 3 laps while it was put right. When Hawthorn returned to the fray he broke the lap record at 115.81mph and would have won had it not been for the delay. As it was Jaguar's honour was ably upheld by the Ecurie Ecosse standard and unmodified D Type driven by Sanderson/Flockhart which had a race long dual with the Aston Martin of Moss/Collins which finished in 2nd place. 3rd was the Ferrari of Trintignant/Gendebien and 4th a further D Type entered by L'Equipe National Belge, driven by Swaters/Rouselle. 5th came a Porsche RS driven by Frankenberg/Rouselle and 6th the Hawthorn/Bueb Jaguar. A Jaguar XK140 driven by Walshaw/Bolton was disqualified after refuelling a lap too early after running in eleventh place. The Aston Martin DBR1 retired in the 24th hour with a damaged rear axle having been running in fourth place at one point. The DB3S driven by Walker/Salvadori crashed and overturned after fifteen hours but, fortunately Walker was not badly injured. Three works Lotus Elevens were driven by Bicknell/Jopp, Allison/Hall and Chapman/Frazer. The first of these finished in seventh place while the others retired during the tenth and twenty-first hours.

1957
A very British Grand Prix

BEFORE THE START of the 1957 Season Mike Hawthorn and Tony Brooks left B.R.M., Hawthorn for Ferrari and Brooks for Vanwall. The 2.5 litre B.R.M. had shown itself to be fast but unreliable and both drivers had not unreasonably described it as being dangerous! Stirling Moss joined Brooks at Vanwall and the two, with the addition of Stuart Lewis-Evans, formed a formidable team. Juan Fangio remained with Maserati where he was supported by Harry Schell, Jean Behra, Maston Gregory and Carlos Menditeguy, while Peter Collins, Luigi Musso and Wolfgang von Trips were with Hawthorn at Ferrari. When the B.R.M.s put in an appearance they were driven by any two of Ron Flockhart, Herbert McKay-Fraser, Roy Salvadori, Les Leston, and Jack Fairman. The Lancia-Ferraris had now lost their side pods altogether so that their exhaust pipes were exposed. They looked fast, powerful and purposeful with wide coloured bands across their nose cowls to identify their drivers. Yet more power was squeezed out of the V8 Lancia engine. A lighter and lower 250F Maserati became available to Juan Fangio and it proved more than a match for the Lancia-Ferraris. Coil springs replaced the leaf springs at the rear of the Vanwalls which had already shown themselves to be highly competitive. Efforts had been made during the winter to improve the road holding of the B.R.M.s. Coil springs were adopted at the rear of the cars in place of the transverse leaf springs while oleopneumatic struts were introduced at the front. The cockpit sides of the B.R.M.s were raised to make the cars more aerodynamically efficient and the power of their engines had been increased. 1957 witnessed the sad demise of Connaught and the appearance of mid engined Cooper-Climax cars in a World Championship event. They would eventually transform the Formula 1 scene.

Peter Collins.

THE WORLD CHAMPIONSHIP SEASON
The Argentine Grand Prix. Buenos Aires: January 13

Stirling Moss was released by Vanwall for the race and so was able to drive one of the new lighter and lower 250F Maseratis in company with Juan Fangio and Jean Behra. Carlos Menditeguy and Joakim Bonnier had 1956 Maseratis while Harry Schell and Luigi Piotti drove works supported entries. Mike Hawthorn, Peter Collins, Eugenio Castellotti and Froilan Gonzales had the new Lancia-Ferraris while Luigi Musso and Cesare Perdisa were given 1956 cars. Alessandro de Tomaso drove a 4 cylinder Ferrari. Maseratis dominated practice with Moss 1.1 seconds faster than Fangio with Behra a further 3 seconds in arrears. The three were joined on the front row of the grid by Castellotti's Lancia-Ferrari, 1.8 seconds slower than Moss. The three Lancia-Ferraris of Collins, Musso and Hawthorn monopolised the second row. The third row was composed of Menditeguy (Maserati), Schell (Maserati), Gonzales (Lancia-Ferrari), and Perdisa (Lancia-Ferrari). The starter failed to give a clear indication as to precisely when the race should get underway, but it was Behra who led followed by Fangio and Castellotti, while Moss spent nine laps in his pit having his throttle linkage repaired. Then Castellotti forced his way to the front for a brief period, followed by Behra and Fangio, and after Behra had recovered his leading position he was relieved of it again on lap 13, this time by Collins. Collins retained the lead for thirteen laps but dropped back to ninth place with a slipping clutch before finally retiring on lap 27. Fangio passed Behra into the lead and behind them were the Lancia-Ferraris of Hawthorn, Musso, and Castellotti whose car had been delayed with a spin. Collins took over Perdisa's car when his own car's clutch had burnt out and then, in turn, handed it on to von Trips after making some progress through the field. Musso and Hawthorn also retired with clutch trouble and Castellotti exited the race on lap 76 after losing a rear wheel. So Maseratis swept the board with Fangio winning at 80.609mph from Behra, Menditeguy and Schell. Then came the Lancia-Ferraris of Gonzales/de Portago, and Perdisa/Collins/von Trips. Seventh and eighth were the Maseratis of Joakim Bonnier and Moss. Moss had driven brilliantly after his long delay and established the fastest lap of the day at 83.580mph. The only other finishers were de Tomaso's Ferrari and Piotti's Maserati.

The Monaco Grand Prix. Monte Carlo: May 19

Sadly Eugenio Castellotti had been killed while testing at Modena and his place was taken at Ferrari by Maurice Trintignant. Stirling Moss (Vanwall), Mike Hawthorn (Lancia-Ferrari), Peter Collins (Lancia-Ferrari) and Tony Brooks (Vanwall) were all equipped

Mike Hawthorn in his Ferrari during practice for the 1957 Monaco Grand Prix.

with potentially race winning cars. Juan Fangio, Carlos Menditeguy and Harry Schell had the new Maseratis, and there were two earlier models for Giorgio Scarlatti and Hans Herrmann. Collins and Hawthorn had the new narrow bodied Lancia-Ferraris while Wolfgang von Trips and Trintignant drove the earlier full width cars. B.R.M.s were driven by Roy Salvadori and Ron Flockhart, both of whom had problems with the brakes and handling of their cars. The Maserati drivers tried a V12 engined car but found it slow to pick up revs. Moss once again won the prize for setting the fastest lap during the first day of practice with his Vanwall, but Fangio's Maserati was at the head of the starting grid of 16 cars on Sunday. Collins was second with the leading Lancia-Ferrari and Moss third in his Vanwall. Immediately behind them came Brooks and Hawthorn. Further down the grid was the lone B.R.M. of Ron Flockhart, and the Connaughts of Stuart Lewis-Evans and Ivor Bueb were 13th and 16th. Salvadori had failed to make the first 16. Jack Brabham had crashed his 2 litre Cooper-Climax and taken over Les Leston's car. Both Collins and Salvadori had fun with the little Coopers before their drivers arrived for practice. Collins crashed Hawthorn's Lancia-Ferrari and this resulted in the 'Farnham Flyer' having to race the spare car.

At the start of the race on Sunday Moss managed to beat Fangio narrowly around the Gasworks hairpin and Collins passed Fangio as he approached the Casino. Fangio recovered his second place and behind Collins came Schell, Brooks, Menditeguy and Hawthorn. Then on lap 4 Moss crashed as he came out of the tunnel into the bright daylight and Collins and Hawthorn, who were close behind, immediately joined him by the harbour wall. All three were out of the race while Fangio and Brooks weaved through the wreckage and proceeded to dominate the race. Behind them came von Trips, Menditeguy and

Stuart Lewis Evans driving the 'Toothpaste Tube' Connaught into 4th place at Monaco.

Brabham, and the last named secured fourth place when Menditeguy stopped to change a wheel. Hawthorn took over von Trips' car only to hand it back when he found the cockpit too cramped for his frame. Menditeguy crashed after getting past Brabham who ran third after the engine of von Trips Lancia-Ferrari blew up. Then the fuel pump failed on Brabham's Cooper-Climax and, as he pushed it towards the finishing line to the sympathetic applause of the crowd, he was passed by Gregory (Maserati), Lewis-Evans (Vanwall) and Trinitignant (Lancia-Ferrari). Fangio won the race at 64.722mph, 25 seconds ahead of Brooks and 2 laps ahead of Gregory. He also recorded the fastest lap of the race at 66.621mph.

The French Grand Prix. Rouen: July 7

There was no Belgian or Dutch Grand Prix in 1957 and the French Grand Prix was held at Rouen, organised by the Automobile Club Normand in place of the Automobile Club du Champagne. Stirling Moss was unwell and Tony Brooks was recovering from the injuries he sustained at Le Mans. Roy Salvadori had transferred his allegiance from B.R.M. to Vanwall and his place at B.R.M. was taken by the young American driver Herbert MacKay-Fraser. The Maseratis of Juan Fangio and Jean Behra lined up at the front of the grid with Luigi Musso's Lancia-Ferrari, while the second row consisted of Harry Schell's Maserati and Peter Collins' Lancia-Ferrari. Then came Salvadori (Vanwall) Mike Hawthorn (Lancia-Ferrari) Maurice Trintignant (Lancia-Ferrari) Carlos Menditeguy (Maserati) Stuart Lewis-Evans ((Vanwall) Ron Flockhart (B.R.M.) MacKay-Fraser (B.R.M.) Jack Brabham (Cooper-Climax) Horace Gould (Maserati) and Johnny McDowell (Cooper-Climax).

All the cars were obliged to be started by means of portable mechanical starters instead of being pushed and this led to great confusion, but it was Musso who led the race from Behra, Fangio, Collins, Schell with, surprisingly, Mackay-Frazer in sixth place. Flockhart's B.R.M. crashed on the second lap and Salvadori dropped back after stopping to have his oil tank cap secured. Fangio passed both Behra and Musso to take the lead, while Collins slowed with gearbox problems. Sadly, Mackay-Frazer's B.R.M. was withdrawn on lap 25, after going strongly and leading the British contingent, when it was thought that his rear universal joint was seizing. It afterwards proved to be a false alarm. Tragically he would be killed in a Formula 2 race the following week. As Fangio continued serenely on his way at the front, the Lancia-Ferraris of Musso, Collins and Hawthorn followed ahead of the Maseratis of Behra and Schell and McDowell's Cooper-Climax. Musso moved into second place and Behra was overtaken by Hawthorn when he was slowed by a damaged exhaust pipe. Brabham took over McDowell's car. So the race was won by Fangio at 100.016mph from the three Lancia-Ferraris of Musso, Collins and Hawthorn. Then came Behra, Schell and the McDowell/Brabham Formula 2 Cooper-Climax nine laps behind the winner. Musso was credited with the fastest lap at 102.767mph.

The British Grand Prix. Aintree: July 20

The British Grand Prix was held at Aintree again in 1957 and Stirling Moss and Tony Brooks were joined again by Stuart Lewis-Evans in the Vanwall team. All three tried Dunlop as opposed to Pirelli tyres because the latter were no longer being manufactured and the remaining stocks were low. The Lancia-Ferraris and B.R.M.s were suffering from under steer and the V12 Maseratis were nowhere to be seen. During practice, Reg Parnell circulated in an Aston Martin DB3S with a camera mounted on board. When the cars lined up to start Behra's Maserati was sandwiched between the Vanwalls of Moss and Brooks at the front of the grid. Juan Fangio and Mike Hawthorn were on the second row and Lewis-Evans, Harry Schell and Peter Collins were in the next row back.

Starting Grid

S. Moss	J. Behra	C.A.S. Brooks
Vanwall	Maserati	Vanwall
2 min 00.2 secs	2 min 00.4 secs	2 min 00.4 secs

J.M. Fangio	J.M.Hawthorn
Maserati	Lancia-Ferrari
2 min 00.6 secs	2 min 01.2 secs

S. Lewis-Evans	H. Schell	P. Collins
Vanwall	Maserati	Lancia-Ferrari
2 mins 01.2 secs	2 mins 01.4 secs	2 min 01.8 secs

M. Trintignant	L. Musso
Lancia-Ferrari	Lancia-Ferrari
2 mins 03.2 secs	2 mins 03.4 secs

C. Menditeguy	L. Leston	J. Brabham
Maserati	B.R.M	Cooper-Climax
2 min 05.4 secs	2 min 05.6 secs	2 min 07.0 secs

H. Gould (Non starter)	R. Salvadori
Maserati	Cooper-Climax
2 mins 07.0 secs	2 min 07.4 secs

J. Fairman	J. Bonnier	F.R. Gerard
B.R.M	Maserati	Cooper-Bristol
2 mins 08.6 secs	2 mins 12.6 secs	2 mins 12.6 secs

I. Bueb
Maserati
2 mins 15.4 secs

Behra led the race at first but Moss was close behind him and took the lead before the end of the first lap. So the crowd watched Moss driving a British car at the front of the pack, which consisted of Behra, Brooks, Hawthorn, Collins, Schell. Moss extended his lead while Hawthorn challenged first Brooks and then Behra, while Fangio was passed by Musso and Lewis-Evans, his engine sounding out of sorts. Then Moss had to surrender a seemingly unassailable lead on lap 22 when he stopped at the pits with engine trouble. On lap 26 Moss took over Brooks' Vanwall, as Brooks was still not fully recovered, and he set off in ninth place while Behra, Hawthorn and Collins were by this time far ahead. Moss had the bit between his teeth and, undeterred by the deficit, climbed to fifth place by lap 45, right up with Collins. Both B.R.M.s retired on laps 45 and 48 with mechanical problems without being able to cope with the Coopers, and Fangio finally retired on lap 49 his engine problems unresolved. Collins withdrew from the race with a fuel leak while Moss continued to close up to the leaders. Then on lap 69 Behra's clutch broke and Hawthorn suffered a puncture from the resulting debris. Lewis-Evans led briefly but was quickly overtaken by Moss and it seemed that it would be a Vanwall one-two. Sadly this was not to be as the throttle linkage broke on Lewis-Evans' car. After a brief stop for 10 gallons of fuel the Brooks/Moss Vanwall won by 40 seconds at a speed of 86.79mph from the Lancia-Ferraris

Jean Behra driving the 'Lightweight' 250F Maserati during the 1957 British Grand Prix at Aintree.

Stirling Moss winning the 1957 British Grand Prix with Tony Brooks' Vanwall, followed by Stuart Lewis Evans.

of Musso and Hawthorn. Next came Trintignant/Collins (Lancia-Ferrari), Salvadori (Cooper-Climax), Gerard (Cooper-Bristol), Lewis-Evans (Vanwall) and Bueb (Maserati). It was the first time a British car had won the British Grand Prix.

The fastest lap of the race was also recorded by Moss at 90.60mph.

Results
1. C.A.S. Brooks/S. Moss Vanwall 3 hr. 06 mins 37.8 secs.
2. L. Musso Lancia-Ferrari 3 hr. 07 mins 03.4 secs.
3. J.M. Hawthorn Lancia-Ferrari 3 hr. 07 mins 20.6 secs.
4. M. Trintignant/P.Collins Lancia-Ferrari 2 laps behind.
5. R. Salvadori Cooper-Climax 5 laps behind.
6. F.R. Gerard Cooper-Bristol 8 laps behind.
7. S. Lewis-Evans Vanwall
8. I. Bueb Maserati 19 laps behind.

Retirements: J. Bonnier Maserati transmission on lap 18, C. Menditeguy Maserati transmission on lap 35, H. Schell Maserati water pump on lap 39, L. Leston B.R.M. engine on lap 45, J. Fairman B.R.M. engine on lap 48, J.M. Fangio Maserati engine on lap 49, S. Moss/C.A.S. Brooks Vanwall engine on lap 51, P. Collins Lancia-Ferrari radiator on lap 53, J. Behra Maserati clutch on lap 69, J. Brabham Cooper-Climax clutch on lap 75.

The German Grand Prix. Nurburgring: August 4

Although Jean Behra had won the non Championship Caen Grand Prix in a B.R.M. at the end of July, there were no B.R.M.s at the Nurburgring. The Vanwalls, Maseratis and Lancia-Ferraris were joined by the 1500cc Porsches of Edgar Barth, Umberto Maglioli, and Carl Godwin de Beaufort, the first of whom was 12th fastest in practice. The Vanwalls were not set up to withstand the battering they were to receive on the demanding Nurburgring circuit and various components became detached from them during practice. At the front of the grid was Juan Fangio (Maserati) Mike Hawthorn (Lancia-Ferrari) Behra (Maserati) and Peter Collins (Lancia-Ferrari). The Vanwalls of Tony Brooks, Stirling Moss and Stuart Lewis-Evans were 5th, 7th and 9th. Hans Herrmann drove a Maserati and was 11th fastest, while Roy Salvadori and Jack Brabham were 14th and 18th in their Formula 2 Cooper-Climax cars.

Mike Hawthorn's Lancia-Ferrari during the German Grand Prix at the Nurburgring.

At the end of the first lap Hawthorn led narrowly from Collins, and behind them came Fangio, Behra, Musso, Schell, Brooks, Moss and Lewis-Evans. On the third lap Fangio took second place from Collins and then passed Hawthorn to lead the race, thereafter drawing away from them. Collins proceeded to overtake his 'mon ami' team mate but neither could catch the flying Fangio. Behra dropped back when he stopped for fuel and tyres while Lewis-Evans spun off and retired with a seized gearbox and a badly bent car. When Fangio pitted on lap 12 for fuel and tyres he lost an inordinate amount of time and re-entered the race 50 seconds behind the fleeing Lancia-Ferraris. Hawthorn and Collins felt secure in the belief that the race was theirs but Fangio set about the task of hauling them in with a succession

Signed painting of Juan Fangio winning the German Grand Prix in his 250F Maserati.

of lap records. He passed first Collins and then Hawthorn on the penultimate lap and finished the race with a lead of 4 seconds! It was one of Fangio's most famous triumphs. Hawthorn and Collins came second and third, Moss was 4th and the Maseratis of Behra, Schell and Gregory 6th 7th and 8th. Brooks' Vanwall was 9th and the Maseratis of Scarlatti and Halford took up the rear in 10th and 11th places. The winner's speed was 88.820mph and his fastest lap was 91.540mph.

The Grand Prix of Pescara. Pescara: August 18

To compensate for the loss of the Belgian and Dutch Grands Prix in 1957 an additional World Championship race was held at Pescara. It took place on tree lined public roads which were closed for the occasion and which passed through villages. The Lancia-Ferraris were officially absent because of a feud between Enzo Ferrari and the Italian Government so that it was a race between the Maseratis and the Vanwalls with the addition of one Lancia-Ferrari which was privately entered by Luigi Musso but enjoyed works support. The front of the grid consisted of Juan Fangio (Maserati), Stirling Moss (Vanwall) and Luigi Musso (Lancia-Ferrari) and behind them were the Maseratis of Jean Behra and Harry Schell. The Vanwalls of Tony Brooks and Stuart Lewis-Evans were 6th and 8th, while Roy Salvadori and Jack Brabham took up the rear with their Cooper-Climax cars.

The race started earlier in the day than usual because of the intense heat and it was Musso who led in the lone Lancia-Ferrari, followed closely by Moss and Fangio. Brooks' race ended on lap 1 with a broken piston. Then Moss took the lead and Musso held on to him while Fangio fell back. Eventually Moss established a firm lead on Musso but Lewis-Evans' Vanwall threw a tread which dropped him right back through the field. Another tyre was shredded soon after he had resumed his race at the back of the field. Moss, Musso and Fangio became increasingly strung out, the three being followed by the Maseratis of Harry Schell, Maston Gregory and Giorgio Scarlatti. On lap ten the lone Lancia-Ferrari's engine seized after oil had leaked from the car so that Musso was out of the race. Fangio lost 3 minutes in the pits after bending a wheel, having spun on Musso's oil, and so Moss won the race unchallenged at a speed of 95.695mph. The Maseratis of Fangio, Schell and Gregory were second, third and fourth, the Vanwall of Lewis-Evans fifth, Scarlatti's Maserati sixth, and seventh was Brabham's Cooper-Climax. The fastest lap of the race was achieved by Moss at 97.876mph.

The Italian Grand Prix. Monza: September 8

B.R.M. had become a spent force by the end of 1957 but the Vanwalls came to Monza for the final race of the Season in fine form. The banked section of the course was not used because of its effects on the tyres in 1956 and the three Vanwalls were fastest in practice, with Stuart Lewis Evans quickest of all. Then came Tony Brooks and Stirling Moss, with Juan Fangio completing the front row in his Maserati. Peter Collins had the only Lancia-Ferrari to make the second row with the Maseratis of Jean Behra and Harry Schell, and behind him were the Lancia-Ferraris of Wolfgang von Trips, Luigi Musso and Mike Hawthorn. Behra was driving the new V12 engined Maserati which was going well at last.

The Vanwalls were out in front at the start of the race in the order of Moss, Lewis-Evans and Brooks but Behra climbed to second place behind Moss at the end of the first lap and he was followed by Lewis-Evans and Brooks. Musso and Behra began to swop the lead with

Peter Collins' Lancia-Ferrari during the Italian Grand Prix at Monza.

B G Apps

each of the three Vanwalls in turn while Fangio kept the five in close company. On lap 20 Brooks was delayed with a sticking throttle and on lap 23 Lewis-Evans was held at his pit for temporary repairs to a cracked cylinder head. Fangio was now in second place but Moss' lead grew by the lap. Behra stopped for fuel and tyres on lap 28 and Brooks made a further stop to remedy an oil leak from his gearbox so that the order became Moss, Fangio, Collins, Behra and Hawthorn. Both Behra and Lewis-Evans experienced engine troubles while Moss was coming close to lapping Fangio! Collins joined the list of retirements with a sick engine and Fangio, after having been lapped, unlapped himself when Moss came in for oil and a new rear tyre. When Fangio stopped for tyres Moss was left with a clear lead so that he was able to ease back and win the race at 120.274mph. Fangio was 42.9 seconds behind in second place, von Trips (Lancia-Ferrari) third, Gregory (Maserati) fourth, Scarlatti/Schell (Maserati) fifth, Hawthorn sixth, Brooks seventh, Musso eighth, Francisco Godia (Maserati) ninth, Horace Gould (Maserati) tenth and Andre Simon/ Ottorino Volonterio (Maserati) eleventh. So the end of the Season was marked by a triumph for Stirling Moss, and his Vanwall became the first British car to win at Monza. The fastest lap of the race was recorded by Brooks at 124.034mph.

The World Championship

Juan Fangio won the World Championship with 40 points. Stirling Moss was second with 25, Luigi Musso third with 16, Mike Hawthorn fourth with 13 and Tony Brooks fifth with 11. Peter Collins shared eighth place with Jean Behra, and Harry Schell. Stuart Lewis-Evans was 12th with 5 points and Roy Salvadori nineteenth with 2 points.

The Monte Carlo Rally was not held in 1957 because of the petrol shortage.

Mille Miglia

The 1957 Mille Miglia promised to be a great contest between Maserati and Ferrari. Maserati had two V8 4.5 litre cars for Stirling Moss and Jean Behra, while Ferrari had a 4.1 litre V12 cars for de Portago and von Trips, Collins and Taruffi had 3.8 litre V12 Ferraris. In addition there was a Ferrari with a Grand Prix engine enlarged to 3.5 litres for Hans Herrmann. Ron Flockhart drove an Ecurie Ecosse D Type Jaguar and there were also Sunbeam Rapiers, a Triumph TR3, an Austin Healey, a Ford Zephyr, a Lotus 1,100, an Aceca and a team of M.G.s. Having just won the Sebring 12 Hour Race there was great disappointment when Behra had to withdraw his entry after an accident while testing his big Maserati the previous day.

Stirling Moss had Denis Jenkinson alongside him once more but much of the interest of the race disappeared less than 10 miles from the start when his brake pedal became inoperable as he prepared to negotiate a fast bend. Thankfully he managed to bring the car safely to a stop. Ferraris were then left in command of the race with von Trips leading

Stirling Moss and Denis Jenkinson in their 450S Maserati before the start of the 1957 Mille Miglia.

Alfonso de Portago before his fatal crash in the Mille Miglia.

Collins and de Portago. Herrmann retired in the sole remaining Maserati when his sump was damaged after hitting something solid. Collins and Taruffi overtook von Trips before Pescara, and Flockhart withdrew because of a loose petrol tank on his D Type. Next Collins retired with a broken rear axle and Taruffi led from von Trips, Olivier Gendebien and Alfonso de Portago. Then tragedy struck as one of de Portago's tyres burst as he was travelling at 170mph on a straight between Mantova and Brescia. The car shot across the road into ditch, killing de Portago, his co driver, and nine spectators. It resulted in this famous road race never being held again. The race was won by the Ferrari of Taruffi and von Trips finished in second place.

Le Mans

Maserati brought three 4.5 V8 cars to Le Mans, one being a Coupe designed by Frank Costin to be driven by Stirling Moss and Harry Schell. In addition there was a 3 litre Maserati. Ferrari had 4.1 litre V12 cars for Peter Collins/Phil Hill and Mike Hawthorn/Luigi Musso and a 3.8 litre car for Stuart Lewis-Evans/Severi. Aston Martin had DB1/300s for Tony Brooks/Cunningham-Ried and Roy Salvadori/Les Leston, and an experimental 3.7 litre DBR2 for P and G Whitehead. The works D Type Jaguars were not at Le Mans in 1957 but there were five private entrants, including those of the highly efficient Ecurie Ecosse team.

The start of the 24 hour race was more like a Grand Prix than an endurance race with Collins streaking ahead in one of the big Ferraris only to have his engine seize. Hawthorn then led in the other 4.1 litre car until it threw a tread. After the first couple of hours the Italian threat had all but disappeared and the Jaguar of Ivor Bueb/Ron Flockhart came through to lead by a comfortable margin, having appeared to have played a waiting game. It stayed ahead until 4 00 p.m the following afternoon. Another Ecurie Ecosse D Type Jaguar came 2nd driven by Sanderson/Lawrence and a D Type driven by Lucas/Brousselet came 3rd. An Equipe National Belge D Type Jaguar driven by Frere/Rousselle was placed 4th and a 3.8 litre model, entered by Duncan Hamilton and driven by Hamilton/Gregory, was 6th. Success once again eluded David Brown as the 3.7 litre DBR2 driven by Peter Whitehead/Graham Whitehead stopped in the eighth hour after running in 19th position. The DBR1 driven by Brooks/Cunningham-Reid retired when Brooks spun and crashed, fortunately without serious injury, at Tertre Rouge after running in sixth place. The second DBR1 driven by Salvadori/Leston retired in the tenth hour when running in 9th place but a privately entered DB3S driven by Colas/Kerguen finished 11th and also won the 3 litre class. A works Lotus Eleven driven by Frazer/Chamberlain finished 9th, a works Lotus Eleven driven by Allison/Hall was 14th, and won both the Index of Performance and the 750cc class. Finally a privately entered Lotus Eleven driven by Hechard/Mason retired in the third hour when it ran out of fuel. The highest placed non British car was the Lewis-Evans/Severi Ferrari which finished in 5th place. It seemed that, even without the works team, Jaguars were still able to retain the role which had been bequeathed to them by Bentley at Le Mans.

1958
A British World Champion at last

THE YEAR 1958 WITNESSED THE replacement of the Lancia-Ferrari by the new Ferrari Dino 246 which owed nothing to the old V8 Lancia D50. It had a V6 engine and was a development of the Formula 2 Dino 156, both cars being named after Enzo Ferrari's son. It had a multi-tubular space frame with coil springs in the front and a De Dion axle with a transverse leaf spring at the back. It was designed to run on the now regulation normal petrol, unlike the Vanwalls and the B.R.M.s which had to be adapted for the purpose at the cost of some loss of power. In 1958 the much loved 250F Maseratis would only be seen in the hands of private entrants as Maserati had withdrawn from motor racing for financial reasons. It therefore fell to Vanwall, B.R.M. and Cooper to provide the new Ferrari with competition. Colin Chapman chose to stay with the front engined configuration for his Frank Costin designed Lotus 16.

Mike Hawthorn.

THE WORLD CHAMPIONSHIP SEASON
The Argentine Grand Prix. Buenos Aires: January 19

There were no less than six privately entered Maseratis in Buenos Aires for the Argentine Grand Prix and two of them were Lightweight 250Fs leased to Juan Fangio's racing manager, Marcello Giambertone and driven by Fangio and Carlos Menditeguy for Scuderia Sud-America. Fangio was fastest in practice and had the new Dina 246 Ferraris of Mike Hawthorn and Peter Collins together with Jean Behra's Maserati alongside him on the starting grid. Then came Luigi Musso's Ferrari, Carlos Menditeguy's Maserati and Stirling Moss, in the absence of the Vanwall team, driving Rob Walker's 1960cc Cooper-Climax. The Maseratis of Harry Schell, Fransciso Godia and Horace Gould completed the small field. It turned out to be an epic race in which the little Cooper-Climax was matched against the might of the 2.5 litre Ferraris. Collins suffered a broken drive shaft on the line and so his race was over before it had begun. It was Behra who led initially but he was soon overtaken by Hawthorn and Fangio and he had Moss in close company. Eventually Moss overtook Behra and, when Hawthorn stopped for an oil check and Fangio stopped to replace a wheel after throwing a tread, Moss led the race in his tiny underpowered Cooper. There was no question of Moss being able to stop for new rubber as his car had bolt on wheels, so he kept an anxious eye on his rear treads. Behra, now in second place, spun and Fangio's engine became less crisp so Moss had the two Ferraris of Musso and Hawthorn behind him, lying second and third but some distance away. His object became one of conserving his tyres until the end of the race while the Ferrari drivers mistakenly believed that Moss would have to stop to replace them. They realised too late that this was not going to happen and their efforts to catch the Cooper were unsuccessful. Moss crossed the line 2.7 seconds ahead of Musso's Ferrari, his tyres worn down to the canvas. Hawthorn was third, Fangio fourth, and the Maseratis of Behra, Schell, Menditeguy, Godia, and Gould completed the finishers in that order. Moss had won at 83.611mph and Fangio had produced the fastest lap of the race at 85.962mph.

The Monaco Grand Prix. Monte Carlo: May 18

The Vanwalls were back at Monaco in the hands of Stirling Moss, Tony Brooks and Stuart Lewis-Evans. The two B.R.M.s were to be driven by Jean Behra and Harry Schell, and the four Ferraris by Luigi Musso, Peter Collins, Mike Hawthorn and Wolfgang von Trips. Two works Cooper-Climax cars were entered for Roy Salvadori and Jack Brabham while Rob

Wolfgang von Trips during practice for the 1958 Monaco Grand Prix.

Jean Behra's B.R.M. leading Tony Brooks' Vanwall at the start of the 1958 Monaco Grand Prix.

Walker's Cooper-Climax was entrusted to Maurice Trintignant. Graham Hill and Cliff Allison both drove front engined Lotus-Climax 16s and there were seven privately entered 250F Maseratis including one driven by Maria Teresa de Filippis. Behra's B.R.M. shone throughout practice but at the end it was Brooks who was fastest followed by Behra and Brabham. Row two consisted of Roy Salvadori and Trintignant, each in a Cooper-Climax, and then came Hawthorn's Ferrari and the Vanwalls of Stuart Lewis-Evans and Stirling Moss. Peter Collins and Luigi Musso shared the fourth row in their Ferraris and behind them were Harry Schell's B.R.M., Wolfgang von Trips' Ferrari and Cliff Allison in the new Lotus. Giorgio Scarlatti (Maserati), Graham Hill, (Lotus-Climax) and Joakim Bonnier (Maserati) completed the grid. Amongst those who failed to qualify were two Formula 2 OSCAs, de Filippis' Maserati, and the privately entered Connaught of B. Kessler.

At the start Salvadori came through from the second row to lead initially but then lost his advantage by going wide and damaging the steering arm of his Cooper-Climax as the pack crowded him. Then it was Behra's B.R.M. that led, followed by Brooks, Brabham and Moss, with Hawthorn climbing to third place in the opening laps. Brooks stopped out on the circuit on lap 22 to investigate a misfire which he cured by tightening one of his plugs but then failed to restart his car. Lewis-Evans had already retired as had Brabham, and the order became Behra, Hawthorn, Moss and Trintignant. Then on lap 27 Behra came into the pits to retire with brake trouble after what had been the finest hour of a B.R.M. in a World Championship race to date. His team mate Schell dropped out of seventh place after a stop to change plugs. Moss overtook Hawthorn to lead on lap 32 but retired six laps later with valve trouble. Trintignant was now second in Rob Walker's Cooper-Climax and he took the lead when Hawthorn's Ferrari stopped with a broken fuel pump. Then Trintignant enjoyed a comfortable lead in the dark blue Cooper-Climax over the Ferraris of Musso, Collins and von Trips, having no difficulty in maintaining his position. The only change in the order was caused by the forced exit of von Trips' Ferrari on lap 91 when its engine seized up. Trintignant led Musso across the line by 20.3 seconds at an average speed of 67.986mph. After Musso and Collins came Brabham's Cooper-Climax, Schell's B.R.M. and Allison's Lotus-Climax. It had been a brilliant start to the Season for Rob Walker. The fastest lap of the race was set by Hawthorn at 69.933mph.

The Dutch Grand Prix. Zandvoort: May 26

The Vanwall team dominated the practice at Zandvoort with Stuart Lewis-Evans, Stirling Moss and Tony Brooks commanding the front row of the grid but the B.R.M.s were also going well and the team was relaxed before the race. B.R.M. was out to demonstrate that Jean Behra's performance at Monaco wasn't a flash in the pan and Behra and Schell were 4th and 7th. The Coventry-Climax engined Coopers of Jack Brabham, Maurice Trintignant and Roy Salvadori were 5th 8th and 9th, Salvadori's car having a 2.2 litre engine. The Climax engined Lotus' of Cliff Allison and Graham Hill were 11th and 13th., and the Ferraris of Mike Hawthorn, Peter Collins and Luigi Musso 6th, 10th and 12th.

Moss, Lewis-Evans and Brooks led away at the start of the race but Brooks was shunted from behind and Schell commandeered third place with his B.R.M. while Behra was relegated to fifth place. Brooks called at his pit to have his car checked and eventually retired on lap 14 with a damaged rear axle. Schell had overtaken Lewis-Evans on lap 12 but Moss was still out in front with an unassailable lead. The real interest lay further back in the field where Hawthorn and Behra fought for fifth place and the other two Ferraris were battling with Allison and Brabham. Collins retired on lap 33 with gearbox trouble and Behra succeeded in passing first Hawthorn and then Salvadori. Lewis-Evans retired on lap 46 with engine trouble which allowed Behra to hold third place behind his team mate. So the result of the race was a convincing win for Moss with the B.R.M.s of Schell and Behra second and

third. Salvadori was 4th, Hawthorn 5th. Allison 6th Musso 7th, Brabham 8th, Trintgnant 9th, Bonnier (Maserati) 10th, and de Beaufort (Porsche) 11th. Moss won the race at 93.926mph and set the fastest lap at 96.100mph.

Stirling Moss winning the Dutch Grand Prix at Zandvoort in his Vanwall on May 26.

The Belgian Grand Prix. Spa: June 15

The Vanwalls of Stirling Moss and Tony Brooks were 3rd and 4th in practice at Spa. Moss' car had wire wheels in front and alloys at the back while the other Vanwall drivers had alloys all round. The Ferraris of Mike Hawthorn and Luigi Musso were 1st and 2nd, while Stuart Lewis-Evans was back in 13th position on the grid with the third Vanwall. The Ferraris now had aluminium air intakes for their Weber carburettors in place of the Perspex ones and Olivier Gendebien's car was painted yellow for Belgian. The B.R.M.s of Harry Schell and Jean Behra were 7th and 9th. Behra had a high speed crash in early practice but his car was repaired in time for the race. The Coopers of Brabham and Salvadori were 8th and 13th and the Lotuses of Allison and Hill 12th and 15th. Of the five privately entered 250F Maseratis the new model bought by Maria Teresa de Filippis from the factory was 19th and last.

As a result of the flag being held at the start of the race for Maston Gregory's Maserati, the Ferraris made poor starts, with Peter Collins' car spraying boiling water, and it was the Vanwalls of Moss and Brooks that led the way. As the result of a missed gear change the leading Vanwall's race was over on the first lap and Gregory's Maserati lasted no longer. Brooks was followed by Collins, Gendebien, Hawthorn and Behra. Collins overtook Brooks and the two swapped the lead until Collins' Ferrari retired, still overheating, on lap 5. Behra went out of the race on the same lap with falling oil pressure. At this stage Brooks held his lead from Hawthorn and Musso but a burst tyre put Musso out on lap 6, fortunately without injury to the driver, so that Lewis-Evans moved up to third place. Hawthorn began to close what had been a long gap for a number of laps but then Brooks was able to build a substantial cushion once more. This was fortunate because Brooks' gearbox seized at La Source and he

Tony Brooks winning his first
major Grand Prix at Spa in his
Vanwall.

Tony Brooks winning his first major Grand Prix at Spa in his Vanwall.

coasted across the line on the very last lap with 20.7 seconds in hand. Hawthorn was second
and Lewis-Evans third. Then came Allison, Schell, Gendebien, Trintignant (Maserati)
Salvadori (Cooper-Climax), Bonnier (Maserati) and de Filippis. The race was won at
129.922mph and Hawthorn established the fastest lap at 132.357mph.

The French Grand Prix. Rheims: July 6

Mike Hawthorn's Ferrari was in pole position at Rheims and alongside it on the front row
of the grid was the Ferrari of Luigi Musso and the B.R.M. of Harry Schell. Then came Peter
Collins (Ferrari), Tony Brooks (Vanwall), Stirling Moss (Vanwall), Maurice Trintignant
(B.R.M.) and Juan Fangio in a brand new Maserati which was the prototype of the T3
Piccolo car.

Schell seized the lead initially but soon Hawthorn passed him and then held it by a

Mike Hawthorn winning the
French Grand Prix at Rheims
in his Ferrari Dino.

widening margin until the end of the race. On lap 2 the order was Hawthorn, Musso, Collins, Brooks, Fangio, Jean Behra (B.R.M.) and Schell, all seven keeping close company. Collins left the road on lap 5 due to a problem with his brake pedal, and five laps later Musso's car slid wide on the bend after the pits and turned over, the driver being thrown out. Tragically this great Italian driver was to die of his injuries. Brooks then took second place until gearbox troubles brought about his retirement on lap 16. Fangio, in a car that was under performing, nevertheless disputed second place with Behra and Moss until he made a brief pit stop. On lap 40 the B.R.M. retired with fuel starvation and the order remained Hawthorn, Moss, Wolfgang von Trips, who had recovered from a poor start, Fangio and Collins. This situation remained constant until the end of the race, Hawthorn winning by a margin of 24.6 seconds at a speed of 125.453mph from Moss, von Trips, Fangio and Collins. He also made the fastest lap of the race at 128.160mph. Jack Brabham was 6th Phil Hill (Maserati) was 7th Joakim Bonnier (Maserati) 8th Gerino Gerini (Maserati) 9th Troy Ruttman (Maserati) 10th and Salvadori (Cooper-Climax) 11th.

British Grand Prix. Silverstone: July 19

It was good to see two Connaughts at Silverstone although both were inevitably outclassed by the more modern machinery. Four makes were represented on the front row of the starting grid in the order of Vanwall (Stirling Moss) B.R.M. (Harry Schell) Cooper-Climax (Roy Salvadori) and Ferrari (Mike Hawthorn). Cliff Allison had the front engined Lotus-Climax on the second row in a highly creditable fifth place. Sadly the Ferrari team were without its Italian ace Luigi Musso. Jack Brabham was 10th in his Cooper-Climax and the Connaughts were 17th (Bueb) and last (Fairman).

Ron Flockhart testing the first Lotus-Climax in 1957.

Graham Hill driving in the Lotus-Climax at Silverstone in the British Grand Prix.

The starting grid

J.M. Hawthorn	R. Salvadori	H. Schell	S. Moss
Ferrari	Cooper-Climax	B.R.M	Vanwall
1 min 40.4 secs	1 min 40.0 secs	1 min 39.8 secs	1 min 39.4 secs

	S. Lewis-Evans	P. Collins	C. Allison	
	Vanwall	Ferrari	Lotus-Climax	
	1 min 41.4	1 min 40.6 secs	1 min 40.4 secs	

W. von Trips	J. Brabham	C.A.S. Brooks	J. Behra
Ferrari	Cooper-Climax	Vanwall	B.R.M
1 min 42 secs	1 min 42 secs	1 min 41.6 secs	1 min 41.4 secs

	G. Hill	J. Bonnier	M. Trinignant	
	Lotus-Climax	Maserati	Cooper-Climax	
	1 min 43 secs	1 min 43 secs	1 min 42.6 secs	

G. Gerini	I. Bueb	I. Burgess	C. Shelby
Maserati	Connaught	Cooper-Climax	Maserati
1 min 53 secs	1 min 51.4 secs	1 min 45.4 secs	1 min 44.2 secs

	A. Stacey	J. Fairman	
	Lotus-Climax	Connaught	
	1 min 58.8 secs	1 min 58.8 secs	

After setting a new lap record in practice, Moss led initially from Schell and Salvadori but at the end of the first lap the order was Collins, Moss, Hawthorn, Schell and Brooks. Collins drew steadily away in the laps that followed and it was clear that no one was going to catch him. Lewis-Evans progressed to fourth place behind Hawthorn. He was well behind the leaders, but ahead of Schell, Brooks and Salvadori. Behra retired after he hit a hare and punctured his tyre on lap 20 and on lap 26 Moss' race ended with a blown engine. Hawthorn came in for oil on lap 44, but when he rejoined the fray he was still in second place while Salvadori and Lewis-Evans disputed third place. The race ended with Peter Collins the clear winner by 24.2 seconds at a speed of 102.05mph, followed by Hawthorn, Salvadori in the 2.2 litre Cooper-Climax, Lewis-Evans, Schell, Brabham, Brooks, Trintignant, and Shelby's Maserati. Hawthorn established the fastest lap of the race at 104.53mph.

Results

1. P. Collins Ferrari 2 hr 09 min 04.2 secs
2. J.M. Hawthorn Ferrari 2 hr 09 min 28.4 secs
3. R. Salvadori Cooper-Climax 2 hr 09 min 54.8 secs
4. S. Lewis-Evans 2 hr 09 min 55.0 secs

Peter Collins winning the British Grand Prix in his Ferrari 246 a week before his fatal crash during the German Grand Prix.

5. H. Schell B.R.M. 2 hr 10 min 19.0 secs
6. J. Brabham Cooper-Climax 2 hr 10 min 27.4 secs
7. C.A.S. Brooks 1 lap behind
8. M. Trintignant Cooper-Climax 2 laps behind
9. C. Shelby Maserati 3 laps behind.

Retirements: J. Fairman Connaught engine on lap 8, G. Hill Lotus-Climax overheating on lap 18, J. Behra B.R.M. suspension on lap 29, A. Stacey Lotus-Climax overheating on lap 20, I. Bueb Connaught gearbox on lap 20, C. Allison Lotus-Climax oil pressure on lap 22, S. Moss Vanwall engine on lap 26, I. Burgess Cooper-Climax clutch on lap 41, G. Gerini Maserati gearbox on lap 50, J. Bonnier Maserati gearbox on lap 50, W. von Trips Ferrari engine on lap 60.

The German Grand Prix. Nurburgring: August 3

There were only two Vanwalls at the Nurburgring because of a shortage of engines and they were second and third in practice in the hands of Tony Brooks and Stirling Moss. Mike Hawthorn's Ferrari was on pole and Peter Collins completed the front row. Wolfgang Von Trips' Ferrari was 5th and Phil Hill's F2 car 10th. B.R.M. had been unable to get to the Nurburgring earlier to test the cars as Harry Schell and Jean Behra had been occupied at Le Mans, and this resulted in their cars being no higher than 8th and 9th in practice. Anthony Marsh drove a Cooper-Climax and was next to Edgar Barth's Formula 2 Porsche in row four. Hanns Herrmann was 20th fastest in a Maserati.

Moss took the lead at the start and was followed by Hawthorn, Collins, Brooks, von Trips, Salvadori and Behra. Then on lap 4 Moss' Vanwall stopped with a faulty magneto so that the race was led by Hawthorn from Collins, von Trips having dropped back after stopping at his pit to report brake trouble. After Hawthorn and Collins came Brooks who gained ground on the Ferraris ahead of him so that the three cars ran close together passing and re-passing each other. Then tragedy struck on lap 11 when Peter Collins left the road at speed and was thrown out as the car somersaulted uncontrolled. Sadly this brilliant and popular British driver died later of his head injuries in hospital. Hawthorn retired shortly afterwards with clutch trouble, and Brooks was left to win the race by a margin of 3 minutes

Stirling Moss in his Vanwall at the Nurburgring during the German Grand Prix.

Tony Brooks winning the German Grand Prix.

Tony Brooks

28.3 seconds and at a speed of 90.309mph from Roy Salvadori's Cooper-Climax. Maurice Trintignant came next, then von Trips and finally Cliff Allison in his Lotus-Climax. Behra had chosen to retire on lap 4, unhappy with his car's performance. Schell retired on lap 9 with no front brakes. Moss recorded the fastest lap of the race at 92.907mph.

Portuguese Grand Prix. Oporto: August 24

Motor Sport described the Oporto circuit as 'a true road circuit and one of the last real street races, containing all the normal hazards of a town, including tram lines, kerbstones, cobbles, drains, trees, lamp posts, pillar boxes and so on'. Signorina de Filippis hit a lamp post in practice and borrowed Gerino Gerini's 250F for the race. The American Carol Shelby drove a Centro Sud Maserati. The pattern of the starting grid presented a combination of Vanwalls, Ferraris and B.R.M.s at or near the front with a supporting cast supplied by Cooper-Climax, Lotus-Climax and 250F Maseratis. Following practice, Stirling Moss (Vanwall) Mike Hawthorn (Ferrari) and Stuart Lewis-Evans Vanwall composed the front row with Jean Behra (B.R.M.) and Tony Brooks (Vanwall) immediately behind. Then came

Wolfgang von Trips (Ferrari), Harry Schell (B.R.M.) and Jack Brabham (Cooper-Climax). Maria de Filippis was again at the back of the grid.

Moss led Hawthorn at the start, and Hawthorn was followed by von Trips, Schell, Lewis-Evans, Behra, Brabham and Brooks. Hawthorn overtook Moss on the second lap and stayed just in front until failing brakes relegated him to second place again on lap 8. Behra was running third in the leading B.R.M. but von Trips, after overtaking Lewis-Evans began to close on him. Brooks spun and was disqualified after being given outside assistance, and Behra moved up to second place when Hawthorn stopped on lap 35 to have his brakes adjusted. Behra was slowed by a faulty plug and he was passed first by Hawthorn and then Lewis-Evans. Moss crossed the line to win at an average speed of 105.029mph but Hawthorn spun on his last lap and had difficulty in re-starting. Stirling came to his aid as he drove by on his victory lap, suggesting that he use the slip road to get his Ferrari going again. Then, after successfully completing his lap Hawthorn was threatened with disqualification. Moss persuaded the officials that no rules had been broken as it had been essential to move the car for reasons of safety, and this generous act of sportsmanship would later cost Moss the World Championship. Following Moss and Hawthorn came Lewis-Evans, von Trips, Schell, Brabham, Trintignant, and Salvadori. The fastest lap of the race was Hawthorn's at 108.742mph.

The Italian Grand Prix. Monza: September 7

The issue at Monza was whether the Vanwalls could beat the Ferraris on their home ground. During practice Stirling Moss' Vanwall had a Perspex bubble which enclosed the cockpit but it was rejected because of the noise it created. He, Tony Brooks and Stuart Lewis-Evans were first, second and fourth in practice and only Mike Hawthorn represented Ferrari on the front row. The three Ferraris of Olivier Gendebien, Wolfgang von Trips and Phil Hill

Tony Brooks (28) Mike Hawthorn (14) and Stirling Moss (30) at the start of the Italian Grand Prix.

came next and the three B.R.M.s of Jean Behra, Harry Schell and Joakim Bonnier were in row three. Graham Hill had his Lotus-Climax in 12th place on the starting grid. Hawthorn's Ferrari had disc brakes and the American Masten Gregory had a brand new 250F Maserati finished in blue and white alongside the three B.R.M.s.

When the flag fell Moss led initially but Phil Hill overtook him in the course of the first lap while both von Trips and Schell were eliminated after a collision in which von Trips was flung from his car, fortunately without serious injury. Hawthorn then passed both Moss and Phil Hill on lap 5 and Phil Hill dropped back after his left rear tyre threw its tread. Hawthorn and Moss continued to battle for the lead while Lewis-Evans, Brooks and Behra were disputing third place. The intense struggle at the front was only resolved when Moss began to experience difficulties with his gearbox and he was forced to retire on lap 18. By this time Hawthorn had an appreciable lead from Behra and Lewis-Evans, while Brooks had stopped to have the cause of oil spraying from the rear of his car investigated. It was due to a split gaiter on his drive shaft and he was able to continue. Bonnier had retired with transmission trouble but Brooks was making progress once more. Lewis-Evans went out with an overheating engine on lap 31 and Behra retired on lap 43 with clutch trouble. It had become a race of attrition but Brooks was up to second place by lap 46 and set after Hawthorn. His task was made easier when the clutch on Hawthorn's Ferrari began to fail and Brooks passed him along the pits straight on lap 60. With ten laps to go the outcome had been resolved if only the Vanwall's tyres could last the distance. Such proved to be the case and it was a particularly sweet victory for Tony Brooks and Tony Vandervell when the Vanwall crossed the line 14.2 seconds ahead of the Ferrari at an average speed of 121.215mph. Phil Hill was 3rd, Gregory/Shelby (Maserati) 4th, Salvadori (Cooper-Climax) 5th Graham Hill (Lotus Climax) 6th and Allison (Lotus-Climax) 8th and last. The fastest lap of the race was recorded by Phil Hill at 124.998mph.

The Moroccan Grand Prix. Casablanca: October 19

The last World Championship Grand Prix of the year was held in Casablanca and while it was still possible for Stirling Moss to win the title the odds were in favour of Mike Hawthorn.

Ferrari brought along a Monza 500 Dino with Girling disc brakes, a F2 car with a Dino 246 engine and alloy front brake drums, and a Dino with Dunlop disc brakes. Gregory had the 1958 lightweight Maserati entered by Scuderia Buell with factory support. For the first time four B.R.M.s were entered for the race and Jean Behra's car was 4th fastest in practice. Of the others, Joakim Bonnier was 8th, Harry Schell 10th and Ron Flockhart 15th. Hawthorn's Ferrari was in pole position with the Vanwalls of Stirling Moss and Stuart Lewis-Evans alongside him. Behra and Phil Hill (Ferrari) were on the second row, Olivier Gendebien (Ferrari), Tony Brooks, his Vanwall with alloy front wheels, and Bonnier on the third. Then came Maurice Trintignant driving Rob Walker's Cooper-Climax and Schell's B.R.M.

With so much depending on the outcome of the race, it was Moss who took an early lead followed by Phil Hill who clung to him until he had to take to the escape road on lap 3. The Ferrari driver lost little time in taking up the chase again and passed both Bonnier and Hawthorn in his pursuit of Moss. On lap 12 Brooks passed Bonnier, who was going extremely well in his B.R.M., and eventually Hawthorn too. This meant that, if the situation remained the same until the end, the Championship title would belong to Moss. The leading Vanwall became battle scarred in the course of lapping Seidel's Maserati but Moss continued undaunted and broke the lap record to consolidate his position. Brooks managed to hold off Hawthorn, which was of course essential for his team mate's success, but retired on lap 30 with a blown engine. It now became necessary for Hawthorn to overtake Phil Hill to gain the World Championship and so the driver of the leading Ferrari was instructed to ease back for Hawthorn to pass. At this time Stuart Lewis-Evans was running in fifth place and on lap 42 his Vanwall's engine blew. As the car left the circuit it caught fire and Lewis jumped out his overalls ablaze. Tragically, he was badly burned and he died in hospital six days later. The result of all this was that the race went to Stirling Moss and the World Championship to Hawthorn. Bonner finished 4th, Schell 5th, Masten Gregory 6th, Roy Salvadori 7th, Jack Fairman (Cooper-Climax) 8th, Hans Herrmann (Maserati) 9th, Cliff Allison (Lotus-Climax) 10th and Gerino Gerini (Maserati) 11th. Moss won the race at 116.461mph and recorded a new lap record at 119.586mph.

The World Championship

Mike Hawthorn won the World Championship with 42 points, Stirling Moss had 41, Tony Brooks 24, Roy Salvadori 15, Peter Collins and Harry Schell 14, Maurice Trintignant and Luigi Musso 12, Stuart Lewis-Evans 11, Phil Hill, Jean Behra and Wolfgang von Trips 9.

The Constructor's World Championship was introduced in 1958 and it was won by Vanwall with 48 points. Ferrari had 40, Cooper-Climax 31, B.R.M. 18, Maserati 6 and Lotus-Climax 3.

Mike Hawthorn winning the Glover Trophy Race at Goodwood in his works Ferrari on Easter Monday 1958.

Monte Carlo Rally

Snow and ice featured strongly in the 1958 Monte Carlo Rally and the competitors who started from Paris experienced the harshest conditions of all. The manufacturer which was best represented amongst all the entrants was Ford with 29 cars. There were 26 Jaguars, 21 Alfa Romeos, 18 Austins, 18 Sunbeams, 16 DKWs, 15 Simcas and 13 Triumphs. 243 cars retired on the roads to Monte Carlo, many of them sliding off the road. Only 59 cars arrived on time and just nine of them without having incurred penalty points. These were then subjected to a 650 mile regularity test, and marks were also deducted for damaged bodywork. The winner was an 845cc Renault Dauphine driven by G Montraisee and J. Feret and "Motor Sport" extolled the virtues of the car, an example of which was owned by the Queen. It also noted that the car could be purchased for £796. 7s and pointed out that

Peter Harper in his Series 1
Sunbeam Rapier during the
1958 Monte Carlo Rally.

Monraisse and Feret winning
the 1958 Monte Carlo Rally in
their Renault Dauphine.

features which were regarded as unconventional in Britain had been
proved by the 1958 Monte Carlo Rally. The Dauphine had a rear
engine with front wheel drive and independent suspension on all
four wheels. Second was a 1290cc Alfa Romeo Giulietta and third
an 896cc D.K.W. The first British car was a Sunbeam Rapier
which finished sixth and the Concours de Confort was won
by Bill Banks with a Rover 105S.

Le Mans

In 1958 the cars were limited to 3 litres so the day
of the big Ferraris was over. David Brown had a
team of DBR1/300s which looked likely to be
the favourites to win. This was borne out by
Stirling Moss who led away in his DBR1 at the
start and proceeded to leave the rest behind.
However his car's engine failed just after 5.00pm,
before it was Jack Brabham's turn to take over. The leader was then von Trips in a Ferrari
followed by Tony Brooks' Aston Martin and Mike Hawthorn's Ferrari. The two Ecurie
Ecosse D Type Jaguars retired with broken pistons soon after the start. As Collins took over
the Ferrari from Hawthorn it rained torrentially and this continued through the hours of
darkness. The Roy Salvadori/Stuart Lewis-Evans Aston Martin skidded in the heavy rain
and crashed out of the race in the fourth hour, while the Brooks/Maurice Trintignant car
retired at 5 50 a.m. with transmission trouble. The Olivier Gendebien/Phil Hill Ferrari took
the lead when the Collins/Hawthorn Ferrari was delayed with clutch trouble. Further back
the Duncan Hamilton/Ivor Bueb privately entered D Type began to advance in the
darkness and the rain until it actually got in front but then Phil Hill passed it again and the
Gendebien/Hill Ferrari went on to win the race. The Hamilton/Bueb Jaguar retired in the
twentieth hour after holding second place. Second place finally went to Graham and Peter
Whitehead's Aston Martin DB3S. Britain was also represented in the race by AC Ace
Bristols, Lister Jaguars, Lotus Elevens and Lotus Fifteens.

1959
The shape of things to come

THE FIRST TWO World Championship events in the 1958 calendar had been won by Rob Walker's 1960cc Cooper-Climax and this raised the question as to whether the more conventional front engined racing cars were soon to be eclipsed. On several occasions the rear, or to be more precise, mid engined, Coopers had put their more powerful rivals to shame. If a Cooper-Climax won the World Championship in 1959 it would surely mark the end of an era as well as a decade, but Enzo Ferrari would be reluctant to surrender to the new trend and Colin Chapman had put his faith in a new front engined Lotus-Climax 16. Added to this, at the beginning of 1959, there was also the front engined Aston Martin DBR4.

It was announced at the end of 1958 that Tony Vandervell had withdrawn from racing for health reasons but another factor must surely have been the death of Stuart Lewis-Evans which had deeply affected him, and there was also the fact that he had achieved his object in 1958. A rear engined Vanwall would make a brief appearance, but it wouldn't compensate for the disappearance of the team of front engined cars. A front engined P25 was loaned to the British Racing Partnership for Stirling Moss to drive in 1959 but the rear engined P48 B.R.M. appeared at the end of the Season. Ferrari equipped his Dino 246 with disc brakes and coil springs and it became the Dino 256. Most significantly, the Coventry-Climax engine was enlarged to 2495cc to enable Coopers to race for the first time on level terms with the other cars.

Jack Brabham.

THE WORLD CHAMPIONSHIP SEASON
The Monaco Grand Prix. Monte Carlo: May 10

The new order was plainly seen on the starting grid at Monaco with Rob Walker's Cooper-Climax in pole position driven by Stirling Moss, and Jack Brabham's works Cooper-Climax was only separated from it by Jean Behra's Ferrari. Rob Walker had brought along a Cooper-B.R.M. as well as a second Cooper-Climax, but the B.R.M. engined car's gearbox was troublesome during practice so the car wasn't used for the race. The Ferraris of Tony Brooks and Phil Hill occupied the second row and behind them were Maurice Trintignant (Cooper-Climax) Joakim Bonnier (B.R.M.) and Roy Salvadori (Cooper-Climax.) The B.R.M.s of Harry Schell and Ron Flockhart formed the fourth row. A Formula 2 Ferrari, driven by Cliff Allison, was 15th fastest, alongside Graham Hill's Lotus-Climax.

It was Behra who led for the first lap of the race from Moss and Brabham followed after

Jean Behra's Dino Ferrari leading Stirling Moss' Cooper-Climax during the 1959 Monaco Grand Prix.

an interval by Phil Hill's Ferrari in fourth place. Wolfgang von Trips (Formula 2 Porsche), Allison and Bruce Halford (Formula 2 Lotus-Climax) were all eliminated by a collision at St. Devote on lap 2. Then Behra's Ferrari was displaced by Moss on lap 21 and by Brabham on lap 22. All was not well under the Ferrari's bonnet and Behra retired on lap 25. Moss was out on his own in front and was followed by Brabham (Cooper-Climax), Schell (B.R.M.) and Brooks (Ferrari), the last two having passed a spinning Phil Hill (Ferrari) at the Casino. Bonnier's B.R.M. retired on lap 45 without brakes and Schell, after spinning on lap 48, was unable to continue. Flockhart's B.R.M. also succumbed to brake troubles on lap 65. Then

Stirling Moss before being robbed of victory by a rear axle failure in Rob Walker's Cooper-Climax at Monaco.

on lap 81 Moss stopped for the source of strange mechanical noises to be investigated and retired on the next lap with a sheared bolt in his final drive. It was left to Brabham to win at 66.711mph with a 20.4 second lead over Brooks who, as he closed the gap in the remaining laps, pushed Brabham to establish a new lap record at 70.072mph. Only six cars finished the race and after Brooks the order was Trintignant (Cooper-Climax), Phil Hill (Ferrari) McLaren (Cooper-Climax) and Salvadori (Cooper-Maserati).

Tony Brooks' Ferrari 246 Dino during the Monaco Grand Prix.

The Dutch Grand Prix. Zandvoort: May 31

Stirling Moss was at Zandvoort the week before the Dutch Grand Prix to put a B.R.M. through its paces while, at the same time, Alfred Owen handed two cars over to the British Racing Partnership which was led by Stirling's father, Leslie and Ken Gregory.

Joakim Bonnier was fastest during practice in his B.R.M. but the Cooper-Climax cars of Jack Brabham and Stirling Moss were second and third. Graham Hill had his Lotus-Climax in 5th place, just 0.1 second slower than Behra's Ferrari, and Maston Gregory was seventh fastest in another Cooper-Climax. Carol Shelby was 10th in the new front engined Aston Martin DBR4/250 and Roy Salvadori was behind him in with the second Aston Martin on the 5th row of the grid.

Bonnier's B.R.M. led away at the start with Masten Gregory's Cooper-Climax, having come up from the third row, right behind him. The Cooper passed the B.R.M. on lap 2 and behind Bonnier were Brooks (Ferrari), Schell (B.R.M.) and Brabham (Cooper-Climax). Brabham passed both Schell and Brooks, and the last two were caught up in a struggle involving, among others, Graham Hill (Lotus-Climax) and Moss (Cooper-Climax). Then Gregory had difficulty in holding his car in gear and Bonnier recovered the lead on lap 12 while Brabham relegated Gregory to third place. Moss overtook Behra and set after Brabham, passing him on lap 46. Schell retired on the next lap with a malfunctioning gearbox. Moss was now hounding Bonnier and, after passing him on lap 60, looked a certain

Joakim Bonnier winning the Dutch Grand Prix for B.R.M. in 1959.

winner until, on lap 63, his gearbox failed. So it was Bonnier's race at an average speed of 93.458mph and, wonder of wonders, a B.R.M. had achieved success in a World Championship Grand Prix at last! The car was followed across the line by Brabham, Gregory, Ireland (Lotus-Climax), Behra (Ferrari), Phil Hill (Ferrari) Graham Hill (Lotus-Climax), Trintignant (Cooper-Climax), Cliff Allison (Ferrari) and Carel Godin de Beaufort (Porsche R.S.K.). Moss had set the fastest lap of the race at 96.990mph.

The French Grand Prix. Rheims: July 5

Stirling Moss drove the British Racing Partnership B.R.M. which was finished in a pale green like the V16 car in its original form and the Pre War works E.R.A.s. Tony Brooks was fastest in practice but Jack Brabham managed to squeeze his Cooper-Climax between his Ferrari and that of Phil Hill at the front of the grid. Moss was fourth alongside Jean Behra's Ferrari and then came Joakim Bonnier (B.R.M.), Masten Gregory (Cooper-Climax) and Maurice Trintignant (Cooper-Climax). Harry Schell and Ron Flockhart were 6th and 9th in their B.R.M.s and Olivier Gendebien was 11th in the third Ferrari. There were three Cooper-Maseratis towards the back of the starting grid driven by Roy Salvadori, Colin Davis and Ian Burgess.

At the start on Sunday afternoon Brooks secured an immediate lead, while Behra stalled, and the order after the first lap was Brooks, Moss, Gregory, Brabham, Phil Hill and Bonnier. Bonnier retired with engine trouble on lap 7 and, by this time, several drivers were being affected by the deteriorating road surface, with sharp stones being thrown up by the rear wheels of the cars in front of them. At 10 laps Brooks still held a comfortable lead but now

Tony Brook's winning the French Grand Prix in his Dino 256 Ferrari having led from the fall of the flag.

it was from Trintignant, Brabham, Moss, and Behra who had recovered from his disastrous start. Trintignant spun and dropped back to a lowly position after calling at his pit. Then it was Phil Hill who battled with Behra for third place behind Brooks and Brabham, but Behra overdid it in his efforts to wrest second place from Brabham and dropped back again. Phil Hill passed Brabham on lap 26 but Behra retired with engine trouble. Now it was the turn of Moss to close first on Brabham and then on Phil Hill, but his engine stalled after he spun at Thillois, already clutchless, and efforts to get him re-started caused his disqualification. Brooks won by 27.5 seconds from his team mate Phil Hill at a speed of 127.430mph. Brabham was 3rd, Gendebien 4th, Bruce McLaren (Cooper-Climax) 5th, Flockhart 6th, Schell 7th, Scarlatti (Maserati) 8th, de Beaufort (Maserati) 9th, Fritz D'Orey (Maserati) 10th, Trinitignant 11th. Moss established the fastest lap of the race in his P25 B.R.M. at 130.045mph.

The British Grand Prix. Aintree: July 18

It was again Aintree's turn in 1959 to stage the British Grand Prix and the two Astons were present with Roy Salvadori and Carol Shelby on hand to drive them. Jack Brabham set pole position but his time was equalled by Salvadori's Aston Martin and the two cars shared the front row of the grid with Harry Schell's B.R.M. The Ferraris were absentees because of an industrial dispute in Italy and, in consequence, Tony Brooks drove a 1959 Vanwall which failed to perform satisfactorily, either in practice or in the race. Shelby was 6th in the second Aston Martin and alongside Moss' British Racing Partnership B.R.M. and McLaren's Cooper-Climax.

Starting Grid

J. Brabham	R. Salvadori	H. Schell
Cooper-Climax	Aston Martin	B.R.M
1 min 58.0 secs	1 min 58 secs	1 min 59.2 secs

M. Trintignant	M. Gregory
Cooper-Climax	Cooper-Climax
1 min 59.2 secs	1 min 59.4 secs

C. Shelby	S. Moss	B. McLaren
Aston Martin	B.R.M	Cooper-Climax
1 min 59.6 secs	1 min 59.6 secs	1 min 59.6 secs

G. Hill	J. Bonnier
Lotus-Climax	B.R.M
2 min 0.0 secs	2 min 0.9 secs

R. Flockhart	A. Stacey	I. Burgess
B.R.M	Lotus-Climax	Cooper-Maserati
2 min 0.2 secs	2 min 02.8 secs	2 min 03.0 secs

J. B. Naylor	J. Fairman
J.B.W Maserati	Cooper-Climax
2 min 03.0 secs	2 min 04.2 secs

C. Bristow	C.A.S. Brooks	I. Bueb
Cooper-Borgward F 2	Vanwall	Cooper-Borgward F 2
2 min 04.4 secs	2 min 04.6 secs	2 min 04.8 secs

H. Herrmann	F. d'Orey
Cooper-Maserati	Maserati
2 min 05.6 secs	2 min 05.6 secs

H. Taylor	D. Piper	P. Ashdown
Cooper-Climax	Lotus-Climax F 2	Cooper-Climax F 2
2 min 05.6 secs	2 min 06.0 secs	2 min 06.2 secs

M. Taylor
Cooper-Climax F 2
2 min 07.0 secs

It was Brabham who led the field away at the start on Saturday and the B.R.M.s of Schell, and Bonnier who had moved up from the fourth row of the grid, could only follow at a discrete distance. They in turn were chased at close quarters by Gregory (Cooper-Climax), Moss (B.R.M.), and the Cooper-Climax cars of Trintignant and McLaren. Neither the Vanwall nor the Aston Martins could stay with the leaders who, behind the rapidly disappearing Jack Brabham, now consisted of Moss and Schell. Trintignant closed up on Schell while Brooks retired on lap 13 with ignition trouble. Further on in the race McLaren overtook both Trintignant and Schell to command third position behind Brabham and Moss who were now on their own. Bonnier retired on lap 38 with a broken throttle linkage,

Stirling Moss in the British Racing Partnership B.R.M. being pursued by Bruce McLaren's Cooper-Climax at Aintree.

Jack Brabham winning the 1959 British Grand Prix in his Cooper-Climax.

while Moss gradually closed on the leading Cooper-Climax, only to be set back again by an enforced stop for tyres. After this Moss began to gain ground rapidly but he had to stop for a nearside rear tyre, allowing McLaren to snatch second place. Moss re-passed McLaren once again but McLaren made it a spirited dual to the end. Jack Brabham won, having led from start to finish, at 89.88mph. The fastest lap of the race was achieved by Moss and equalled by McLaren at 92.31mph.

Results

1. J. Brabham Cooper-Climax 2 hr 30 mins 11.6 secs
2. S. Moss B.R.M. 2 hr 30 min 33.8 secs

 3. B. McLaren Cooper-Climax 2 hr 30 min 34 secs
 4. H. Schell B.R.M. 1 lap behind
 5. M. Trintignant Cooper-Climax
 6. R. Salvadori Aston Martin
 7. M. Gregory Cooper-Climax 2 laps behind
 8. A. Stacey Lotus-Climax 4 laps behind
 9. G. Hill Lotus-Climax 5 laps behind
10. C. Bristow Cooper-Borgward
11. H. Taylor Cooper-Climax F 2 6 laps behind
12. P. Ashdown Cooper-Climax F 2

Retirements: C.A.S. Brooks Vanwall ignition on lap 13, M. Taylor F2 Cooper-Climax Transmission on lap 16, J. B. Naylor J.B.W.Maserati transmission on lap 18, D. Piper F2 Lotus-Climax overheating on lap 20, H. Herrmann Cooper-Maserati clutch on lap 21, I. Burgess Cooper-Maserati transmission on lap 32, J. Fairman Cooper-Climax gearbox on lap 37, J. Bonnier B.R.M. throttle linkage on lap 38, R. Flockhart B.R.M. spin on lap 54, F d'Orey Maserati crash on lap 57, C. Shelby Aston Martin ignition on lap 69.

The German Grand Prix. Nurburgring: August 2

The Ferraris were back for the German Grand Prix which was held at the fast Avus circuit with its steeply banked curves. It was run in two Heats, the survivors from the first competing again in the second, and the arrangement made allowance for the expected high rate of wear and tear on the tyres. Tony Brooks celebrated the return of the Ferraris by gaining pole position for the first heat. The Cooper-Climax cars were seen to take advantage whenever possible of the Ferraris' slip stream and Stirling Moss was next to Brooks, having come second in practice in Rob Walker's Cooper-Climax. Then came Dan Gurney's Ferrari and, completing the first row of the grid, Jack Brabham's works Cooper-Climax. In the second row were Masten Gregory (Cooper-Climax) Phil Hill (Ferrari) and Joakim Bonnier (B.R.M) and then came Harry Schell (B.R.M), Bruce McLaren (Lotus-Climax), Graham Hill (Lotus-Climax) and Hans Herrmann (B.R.P B.R.M). Cliff Allison had recorded the fastest time of all in his Ferrari but he started back in 14th place instead of on pole because he was only a reserve driver. Sadly Jean Behra had been killed the day before the race in a sports car race when driving a Porsche R.S.K. He had been thrown out of his car when it spun and was instantly killed when he struck a flag pole. A minute's silence was kept in his memory before the start of the Grand Prix.

At the end of the first lap the order was Brooks, Gregory, Moss, and Brabham, but Moss stopped on the second lap with a stripped transfer gear. Allison followed him into retirement on the next lap when his clutch failed. Gregory led for a while in the Cooper-Climax but Brooks soon recovered his position and Gurney lay third. Gurney then passed Gregory but the little Cooper was still able to keep up with him in the high speed chase. Brabham, on the other hand, was forced to retire also with a stripped transfer gear. Meanwhile Phil Hill dropped back. Then Gregory's Coventry Climax engine cried "Enough" and the three Ferraris of Brooks, Gurney and Phil Hill were on their own. Bruce McLaren was fourth in his Cooper-Climax ahead of Schell's B.R.M., and Trintignant's Cooper-Climax was sixth ahead of the B.R.M.s of Bonnier and Herrmann. Ian Burgess was ninth, two laps down and last, in a Cooper Maserati.

The survivors lined up for the Second Heat, their grid positions being decided by their finishing order in the First Heat, and this put Brooks, Gurney, Phil Hill and McLaren on the front row. After a brilliant start by McLaren the three Ferraris overtook him and settled down in the front. Herrmann's B.R.M. crashed at high speed and destroyed itself when its

Tony Brooks' winning the 1959 German Grand Prix.

brakes failed on lap 7 but, miraculously, its driver was not seriously injured when he was thrown clear. McLaren retired on the same lap with what seemed to have emerged as the Cooper-Climax Achilles' heal, and the Ferraris crossed the line in the order of Brooks, Phil Hill and Gurney, followed by Trintignant (Cooper-Climax), Bonnier (B.R.M.), Burgess (Cooper-Maserati) and Schell (B.R.M.). Brooks won the First Heat at 146.67mph and the Second at 140.16mph. The fastest lap of the race was also posted by Brooks at 149.13mph.

The Portuguese Grand Prix. Lisbon: August 23

The Lisbon circuit was of course infinitely better suited to the Climax engined cars than Avus, and Stirling Moss, Jack Brabham and Masten Gregory had the front row of the grid to themselves. Then came Maurice Trintignant's Cooper-Climax and only after this the first front engined car, which was Joakim Bonnier's B.R.M. The Ferraris of Dan Gurney, Phil Hill, and Tony Brooks were 6th , 7th and 10th fastest, the B.R.M.s of Harry Schell and Ron Flockhart 9th and 11th , and the Aston Martins of Roy Salvadori and Carol Shelby 12th and 13th. The Lotus-Climax cars of Graham Hill and Innes Ireland took up the rear in 15th and 16th places after arriving too late to put in many laps.

Moss, in Rob Walker's Cooper-Climax, got in front of Brabham and Gregory half way round the first lap to lead the race while Bonnier's B.R.M. was at the back of the field, its engine having cut out at the start. On lap 6 Graham Hill's Lotus-Climax was hit by Phil Hill's Ferrari as the American, in making up for lost time after a spin, ran into the rear of the Englishman's car when it also spun. Moss left the rest behind as he established an unassailable lead from Brabham, Gregory and McLaren, and then Brabham's car hit a telegraph pole, throwing the driver to safety before destroying itself. Such was Moss' lead that he slowed to tell the Cooper pit that Brabham was alright! Moss finished, a clear winner, at a speed of 95.316mph, from Gregory (Cooper-Climax), Gurney (Ferrari), Trintignant (Cooper-Climax), Schell (B.R.M.), Salvadori (Aston Martin), Flockhart (B.R.M.), Shelby (Aston Martin), Brooks (Ferrari) and Mario Cabral (Cooper-Maserati). Brooks' Ferrari was down on power throughout the race and the Aston Martins were never in contention with the leaders. *Motor Sport* commented, perhaps a little wistfully, that the Aston Martins were 'beautifully made and a credit to any starting grid'. The fastest lap went to Moss at 97.297mph.

The Italian Grand Prix. Monza: September 13

B.R.M. brought a new and experimental mid engined car to Monza but didn't use it in the race. The Italians breathed a sigh of relief when they saw that Tony Brooks had put one red Ferrari on the front row of the starting grid, but it was Stirling Moss who was on pole in the Rob Walker Cooper-Climax, now with knock on rear wheels. Jack Brabham was on Brooks' other side in a works Cooper-Climax. The Ferraris of Dan Gurney, Phil Hill, Olivier Gendebien and Cliff Allison were 4th, 5th , 6th, and 8th. The two Aston Martins of Roy Salvadori and Carol Shelby, still well off the pace, were only 17th and 19th .

The prototype rear engined B.R.M. driven by Harry Schell when it appeared briefly before the 1959 Italian Grand Prix.

After leading initially, Brooks' race came to a sudden end when his engine lost a piston on the first lap. Moss then led from Phil Hill and Brabham, but the American's Ferrari overtook Moss, and the Ferraris of Gurney and Allison eventually got past Brabham too. McLaren retired on lap 23 with a blown engine while the three cars at the front took turns to lead the race. Then on lap 33 Phil Hill brought his car in for new tyres and he was followed in turn by Gurney, Allison and Gendebien. This left Moss, who had been conserving his tyres, clear of the field and the Ferrari team was once again mistaken in believing that his too would have to be replaced before the end of the race.

Moss won by a margin of 46.7 seconds at the record speed of 124.384mph from Phil Hill (Ferrari), Brabham (Cooper-Climax), Gurney (Ferrari), Allison (Ferrari), Gendebien (Ferrari), Schell (B.R.M.), Bonnier (B.R.M.), Trintignant (Cooper-Climax), Shelby (Aston Martin), Davies (Cooper-Maserati), Scarlatti (Cooper-Climax), Flockhart (B.R.M.), Burgess (Cooper-Climax), and Guilio Cabianca (Maserati).
Phil Hill set the fastest lap of the race at 128.111mph.

The United States Grand Prix. Sebring: December 12

The starting grid for the last World Championship race to be held in the 1950s was dominated by the Coventry-Climax engined Coopers which monopolised the front row at Sebring in the order of Stirling Moss, Jack Brabham and Harry Schell. Tony Brooks had the first of the Ferraris in fourth place and then, after Maurice Trintignant's Cooper-Climax came the Ferraris of Wolfgang von Trips, Cliff Allison and Phil Hill. Bob Said had an old 'Toothpaste-tube' Connaught in 13th place. Fritz d'Orey was 17th in a Tec-Mec and Roger Ward was 19th and last in a Kurtis-Kraft. John Cooper disclosed in his book *John Cooper Grand Prix Carpet-Bagger* that Schell had only beaten Brooks' time by discovering a short cut!

Brabham led for a brief spell before being overtaken by Moss who then proceeded to draw away from him. The Connaught spun with a seized engine on the first lap and von Trips shunted Brooks, causing him to stop briefly at his pit. The order on lap 3 was Moss, Brabham, Bruce McLaren, Phil Hill, Innes Ireland (Lotus-Climax) Trintignant (Cooper-Climax), Allison (Ferrari), and Roy Salvadori (Cooper-Maserati). Then on lap 5 Moss, who was still out in front, stopped with transmission problems so that Brabham inherited the lead, followed by McLaren and Allison. Schell, unsurprisingly, failed to match his practice time and retired on lap 6 with a worn out clutch. Phil Hill also retired on lap 9 with clutch trouble and the midget Kurtis–Kraft, looking extremely odd amongst the Formula 1 cars, retired on lap 21 for the same reason. Allison's race was also ended through clutch trouble and Salvadori's Cooper-Maserati retired on lap 24 with a broken transmission. The last few laps witnessed an exciting duel between the Coopers of Brabham, McLaren and Trintignant, surely pointing the way in which Formula 1 would go in the next decade. It was Bruce McLaren who crossed the line first just 0.6 seconds ahead of Trintignant, with Brooks in 3rd place with the fast but almost venerable looking Ferrari. Brabham was 4th, having pushed his car across the finishing line when it ran out of fuel, Ireland (Lotus-Climax) was 5th, von Trips (Ferrari) 6th, and Harry Blanchard (Formula 2 Porsche R.S.K.) 7th and the last to finish. McLaren won at 98.83mph. The fastest lap of the race was set by Trintignant at 101.19mph.

The World Championship

The 1959 World Championship was won by Jack Brabham with 31 points. Then came Tony Brooks with 27, Stirling Moss with 25½, Phil Hill with 20, Maurice Trintignant with 19, Bruce McLaren with 16½, Dan Gurney with 13, and both Joakim Bonnier and Masten Gregory with 10.

Cooper-Climax won the Constructors' Championship with 40 points, followed by Ferrari with 32, B.R.M. with 18 and Lotus-Climax with 5.

Roy Salvadori on his way to second place in the 1959 International Trophy Race at Silverstone in the new Aston Martin DBR4/250.

The Monte Carlo Rally

The weather for the 1959 Monte Carlo Rally was relatively kind to the 322 entries, which included 23 Fords and 23 Citroens. 184 arrived in Monte Carlo within the time stipulated. 168 of these were able to take part in the Final Test of which 119 completed it within the prescribed time. French cars took the first four places, two of them being Citroen ID19s, and the winner was the Citroen ID19 of Collettari and Alexandre. Second was the Simca P60 of Thomas and Delliere, third the DB Panhard of Surles and Piniers and fourth the Citroen ID19 of Marang and Badoche. The first British car, a Sunbeam Rapier driven by Adams and McMillen was fifth. The Ladies' Prize went to Pat Moss/Ann Wisdom in an Austin A40.

Le Mans

The V12 3 litre Ferraris were much faster than the Aston Martins in practice and looked certain to win the race. However, taking lessons from Mercedes Benz, John Wyer ran a tactical race, allowing only Moss and Fairman the freedom to run at their own speed. The other two cars were strictly limited to race to predetermined lap times, with Trintignant and Frere instructed to lap 2 seconds slower than Salvadori and Shelby.

At the start of the race Moss led away followed by the Ferraris of Gendebien, Silva Ramos and Behra. It proved to be impossible for Moss to hold Behra back and so he conceded his lead while the other two Ferraris continued to follow him. Then the leading Ferrari, now driven by Phil Hill retired with carburettor problems while Moss' Aston Martin's engine dropped a valve. The Behra/Gurney Ferrari then led, followed by the Ecurie Ecosse D Type Jaguar of Ireland/Gregory and, by this time, the Salvadori/Shelby Aston Martin had climbed to 3rd place. The leading Ferrari had to stop for repairs to its lights and the Jaguar's engine blew up, so the leading Aston Martin was now at the front of the field. The Aston Martin of Trintignant/Frere moved up to 4th place when the Bueb/Halford Lister Jaguar succumbed to engine trouble. The Salvadori/Shelby Aston had a lengthy pit stop at 2.00am to replenish its fuel, tyres and brake pads, and this placed it a lap down on the Gendebien/Hill Ferrari which now led. The situation on Sunday morning was that the lone Ferrari led the two Aston Martins and appeared to be uncatchable. Then at 11 00 a.m. the Italian car called at its pit with an overheated engine and, after being sent out again, retired at 11 45 a.m as topping up its cooling would have breached the rules. So the Aston Martins of Salvadori/Shelby and Trintignant/Frere finished in first and second places, and the perseverance of David Brown at Le Mans over so many years was richly rewarded. All four cars to finish after the two Aston Martins were G.T. Ferraris.

Roy Salvadori winning the Le Mans 24 Hour Race in an Aston Martin DBR1.

THE END OF
THE DECADE

DECEMBER 31st 1959 marked the end of a decade and also the end of an era because in many respects the 1950s had a character of its own which would be lost with the coming of the 'Swinging Sixties'. Time never stands still or falters for a second even when the clock strikes twelve, and in motor racing there was a continuous process of evolution throughout the 50s and into the 60s. The sport would become progressively less dangerous, in large measure due to the efforts of Jackie Stewart, although, sadly, in the 1960s there would be the tragic deaths of Harry Schell, Chris Bristow, Alan Stacey, Wolfgang von Trips, Jim Clark, Lorenzo Bandini, Mike Spence, and others. Front engined racing cars from

Phil Hill during the Belgian Grand Prix at Spa in his Dino 246 Ferrari on June 19 1960.

Ferrari, Aston Martin, Maserati, Lotus, Scarab and Vanwall continued to feature in 1960, and yet the Ferrari Dino of Phil Hill was the only example to win a World Championship race, this being the Italian Grand Prix at Monza. In 1961 the four wheel drive Ferguson-Climax P99 appeared in the British Grand Prix and was driven by Stirling Moss and Jack Fairman, but the car with which Phil Hill won the World Championship was the new rear engined Tipo 156 Ferrari. Cockpits would become progressively less open, helmets more concealing, and straw bales were banned altogether. Thankfully the cars from the 1950s would continue to be seen at the Goodwood Revival and at other vintage racing car meetings at Silverstone and elsewhere right up to the present day. My only plea is that on such occasions the drivers should be allowed at some point in the programmes to circulate at moderate speed wearing the kit that was worn back in those far off days, if only for the cameras. We are also fortunate in having the Racing Car Museum at Donington Park and the National Motor Museum at Beaulieu. Above all, those of us of a certain age still have our memories of Stirling Moss in a Cooper 500 and a 250F Maserati 250F, Tony Brooks in a Vanwall and a Ferrari Dino 246, and Archie Scott Brown a B Type Connaught and a Lister Jaguar, and all the many others. The sight and sound of the Mark 1 V16 B.R.M. with Juan Fangio at the wheel is unforgetable. There are also memories of the sweet smell of alcoholic fuel which probably made us all a little high, and the very special atmosphere of crowds of spectators, many of them enthusiasts with their young families, enjoying a day at the races. The truth is that races on airfield circuits were a poor substitute for the Continent road circuits but they were all we had and they offered excellent vantage points for the spectators who didn't have as long to wait for the cars to come round as they would have done at the Nurburgring. The Goodwood Nine Hours races were never very popular, which was a pity because they contained most of the excitement of Le Mans, with the cars racing through the hours of darkness, and in a more manageable time frame. The 1950s was still the era of the amateur who raced for the fun of it while also approaching it with sufficient technical know-how and an appropriate resolve to win. Professionalism took over increasingly in the 1960s and this aspect of motor racing, coupled with the spiralling sums of money involved, has advanced progressively ever since. Yet at the end of 1959 we had still to discover Jim Clark, Jackie Stewart, Nigel Mansell, Michael Schumacher, and all the rest. There was no danger of motor racing losing its appeal.